The Trial of Galileo

Essential Documents

The Trial of Galileo

Essential Documents

Translated and Edited by

Maurice A. Finocchiaro

Hackett Publishing Company, Inc.
Indianapolis/Cambridge

17 16 15 14   1 2 3 4 5 6 7

For further information, please address
  Hackett Publishing Company, Inc.
  P.O. Box 44937
  Indianapolis, Indiana 46244-0937

  www.hackettpublishing.com

Cover design by Brian Rak
Composition by Aptara, Inc.

Library of Congress Cataloging-in-Publication Data
The trial of Galileo : essential documents / translated and edited by Maurice
A. Finocchiaro.
  pages cm
  Includes bibliographical references and index.
  ISBN 978-1-62466-132-7 (paperback) — ISBN 978-1-62466-133-4 (cloth)
  1. Galilei, Galileo, 1564–1642—Trials, litigation, etc. 2. Religion and
science—Italy—History—17th century—Sources. 3. Catholic Church—
Italy—History—17th century—Sources. 4. Trials (Heresy)—Italy—
History—17th century—Sources. 5. Inquisition—Italy—History—17th
century—Sources. I. Finocchiaro, Maurice A., 1942–
  QB36.G2T75 2014
  520.92—dc23   2013048853

Contents

Chapter 5
Later Proceedings: Condemnation of Galileo   119

Chapter 6
Reports and Responses: Implementation of Sentence   140

Preface

The trial of Galileo is one of those episodes in world history that have perennial interest and universal significance. The explanation of this fact is not hard to fathom: the episode involved, on one side, the troubles and tribulations suffered by someone whose scientific contributions enabled him to become recognized, by scientists themselves, as the "father of modern science"; on the other side, the episode concerned the actions of an institution—the Catholic Church—which is one of the world's great religions as well as the oldest organization on earth; thus, here we have a classic example of an encounter between science and religion, regardless of how this encounter is further specified. That is, independently of whether the episode is viewed, in the words of a sensationalist slogan, as "the greatest scandal in Christendom" (Koestler 1964), it provides abundant material from which to learn about the nature and the history of science, the nature and the history of religion, and their relationship (whether it is one of conflict, harmony, separation, dialogue, integration, subordination, etc.). It follows that every educated person should be able to form an intelligent opinion of the trial, based on some knowledge, understanding, and assessment of relevant facts, problems, and issues.

This judgment led me, some three decades ago, to collect, translate, and edit the most important documents pertaining to this pivotal episode. I wanted to introduce and annotate these documents in such a way that they could be not only appreciated and utilized by specialized scholars, but also read and understood by intelligent and educated laypersons. This was meant to fill a cultural lacuna that existed not only in the English-speaking world, but also in all other languages, including Italian, which is the language in which almost all the relevant documents were written (a few others were written in Latin). Moreover, I wanted to present the documents in a balanced, impartial, and judicious manner that would avoid one-sidedness and exaggeration, so that readers could make up their own minds and reach their own conclusions. These were the motivations that led me to publish, in 1989, *The Galileo Affair: A Documentary History*.

As expected, that book met with a certain amount of success. Reviewers were unanimous and enthusiastic in their praise. The journal *Nature* (5 October 1989) stated that "it is only now that we can steep ourselves in the atmosphere of the incident and read the very words of the main protagonists, often from their own secret correspondence or from private Inquisition papers. For the first time all the relevant documents are made available in

English in Maurice Finocchiaro's marvellous translation." The London *Times Higher Education Supplement* (3 August 1990) told its readers that the book "provides an invaluable source for English-reading students of 17th-century intellectual history. It is an extremely well-conceived project that will open up the issues to a much wider audience." The *Catholic Historical Review* (1990) called it "an unprecedented achievement . . . The book is imaginatively conceived, assiduously researched, clearly written, and aesthetically produced." And the official journal of the History of Science Society (*Isis*, 1992) found it to be "an intelligently selected and impeccably translated range of documents" which "will facilitate and enrich the teaching of graduate and undergraduate seminars on Galileo, the Scientific Revolution, and the relationship between science and religion."

Thus, the book is still in print, in both paperback and electronic editions. Significantly, it has also been reprinted as a volume of the Notable Trials Library, which publishes its books bound in leather and embossed in gold. And in this connection, it is worth quoting some revealing words of the series' chief editor, Alan Dershowitz (1991), who wrote a brief introduction to this edition: "*The Galileo Affair* should be required reading for everyone who values freedom and fears censorship. The extraordinary virtue of this collection of documents edited by Maurice A. Finocchiaro is that it presents both sides of the dispute."

Obviously, I am the last person to want to diminish the value of my earlier brainchild. Nevertheless, lately I have come to feel the need for a smaller collection of documents for contexts, situations, and courses when less time and space are available than is required to digest the relatively bulky *Galileo Affair*. In fact, its 80 documents amount to about 110,000 words, or 250 printed pages, which together with the critical apparatus of notes, introduction, etc., make up a book of about 165,000 words, or 400 pages. It should be possible to select from these the documents that are more important and more crucial, as compared to the rest. The selected documents may be labeled "essential," and they are the focus of the present book.

Admittedly, an explicit definition of "important" is hard to formulate, and particular judgments of importance are not easy to make. However, importance is a relative notion, as one can see from the fact that my earlier book is itself a selection of the most important documents, relative to all the available documents, published in the twenty volumes of the critical edition of Galileo's complete works (Galilei 1890–1909), plus a few other sources. Thus, the present task of selecting the essential documents of Galileo's trial should be no more difficult than the earlier task of choosing the most important ones.

Furthermore, since I published my earlier collection, I have come to realize that it embodies a few minor oversights that can be easily corrected. One is that my earlier documentary history stops with the Inquisition's sentence and Galileo's abjuration, which occurred on 22 June 1633 and concluded the formal court proceedings. This was, of course, an obvious and natural stopping point. However, besides being pronounced, the sentence had to be implemented, and as with any other trial, such implementation could be carried out in various ways and to varying degrees. Since Galileo lived nine more years, we can expect some of the developments during that final period to be of interest and relevance.

In fact, some of those final reports and reactions are of crucial importance. For example, some of those documents easily and clearly dispel the prison myth—that Galileo spent the last years of his life in prison. This is a view that arose immediately and persisted for centuries, for the simple reason that the sentence mentions imprisonment as part of the punishment. However, documents discovered and published later (such as §31) make clear that this penalty was immediately commuted to house arrest. On the other hand, in some ways the Church remained intransigent and never pardoned Galileo, even when the petition (§32) came from a world-renowned French intellectual and politician who was a friend of the pope's family.

I am *not* saying that the trial of Galileo should be conceived as including the whole series of developments which began with his condemnation in 1633 and continue to our own day, and which make up a cause célèbre of modern Western culture. That is a controversy *about* the original episode, e.g., about whether Galileo's condemnation was right and whether it proves the incompatibility between science and religion. That subsequent and ongoing controversy is also important and instructive, but is not the subject of the present book. I have examined it in another work, *Retrying Galileo, 1633–1992*, published in 2005. For our present purposes, the main thing to keep in mind is that researching that work convinced me of the importance of the post-condemnation period of his life (1633–1642), even from the point of view of the original episode that makes up the trial of Galileo. Thus, it is from that work that I have taken all but the last one of the documents dealing with the implementation of the sentence (§29–§33).

The present book also corrects my earlier omission of a few crucial documents from the 1616–1633 period (§12, §14, and §25). These are simply too revealing and emblematic to be left out. My English translation of these documents is published here for the first time. One of these (§14) is especially significant. Let me explain.

An essential aspect of the trial of Galileo was the legal proceedings. Thus, chapters 3 and 5 of the present book contains the most important legal documents. However, note that the concept of *law* was and remains ambiguous in various ways. For example, what is legally pertinent in twenty-first-century North America obviously cannot be equated to what was legally pertinent in seventeenth-century Italy. Similarly, what was legally relevant according to ecclesiastic or canon law in seventeenth-century Rome may or may not correspond to what was legally relevant according to international law in seventeenth-century Venice. To underscore this second point (but also because of its intrinsic importance), I am adding to the present collection a legal opinion (§14) solicited by the government of the Republic of Venice and written by Paolo Sarpi, an important figure in his own right; it outlines a procedure to render legally valid in Venice the Index's decree of 1616, in light of the 1596 treaty between the Venetian Republic and the Holy See. Thirdly, even the Inquisition's legal proceedings in Rome could be more or less formal, depending on whether they occurred in or out of court; for example, one of the most crucial legal documents is a 1633 letter (§21) by one official to another reporting on his attempt "to deal extra-judicially with Galileo."

Moreover, although the trial of Galileo was in part a legal episode, it would be a mistake to consider it primarily or exclusively a legal episode, as some authors are inclined to do (e.g., Mayer 2012). To do so would be one-sided, and it would deprive the episode of its perennial interest and universal significance; these derive from the intellectual and philosophical issues the trial embodied, and from its human, social, political, bureaucratic, and cultural ramifications and repercussions. One of these essential intellectual issues was the theological (but also methodological) problem of the relationship between Copernicanism and Scripture: not only the question of the logical force of the scriptural argument against Copernicanism (§1), but also the question of its historical soundness—historical in the sense of the past history of theology and biblical hermeneutics and the future development of scientific knowledge (§2). There was also the cluster of epistemological issues about the role of hypotheses, instruments of calculation, and probable reasoning in the search for demonstrated truth of reality (§3–§4). Similarly, chapters 4 and 6 are in part intended to document the repercussions that immediately followed the two phases of legal proceedings.

In short, the present book contains English translations of the most important documents that are essential for an educated person to form an intelligent opinion on the trial of Galileo.

Acknowledgments

The documents translated and edited in this work are being reprinted here mostly from the following much larger book, which I created many years ago: Maurice A. Finocchiaro, *The Galileo Affair: A Documentary History*, © 1989 by the Regents of the University of California, published by the University of California Press. This applies specifically to the documents that in the present volume bear the following numbers: §1, §2, §3, §4, §5, §6, §7, §8, §9, §10, §11, §13, §15, §16, §17, §18, §19, §20, §21, §22, §23, §24, §26, §27, and §28. These twenty-five selections represent about a third of the documents included in that earlier book. Formal permission by the University of California Press is hereby gratefully acknowledged.

Another smaller group of translated documents is reprinted from my *Retrying Galileo, 1633–1992*, © 2005 by the Regents of the University of California, published by the University of California Press. These are the documents here numbered §25, §29, §30, §31, §32, and §33. Again, formal permission by the University of California Press is hereby gratefully acknowledged.

Furthermore, the previously published documents are reprinted here with a few minor revisions or changes. These are usually so small that they are made without note; for example, in the correspondence, almost all salutations, greetings, and signatures have been omitted, as redundant and repetitive in the present context. However, occasionally my translation has been improved as a result of suggestions from other scholars, and then appropriate references are given. On the other hand, the earlier annotations are completely reworked, mostly by significant simplifications and by slight updating. Similarly, although the Introduction to this volume is along the lines of the one found in my *Galileo Affair*, it has been simplified, updated, and refocused. The same holds for other parts of the critical apparatus, specifically the Glossary and the Bibliography.

Other acknowledgments are certainly in order. The prefaces to those earlier books mention the many scholars to whom I am indebted, and a few must be singled out here. For constant support, I am grateful to John Heilbron, who has since published his own *Galileo* (2010); to William Wallace, whose many Galilean works admirably combine historical erudition, philosophical analysis, and Catholic piety; and to Robert Westman, who has finally published his own magnum opus, *The Copernican Question* (2011). For long-standing encouragement and feedback, I also thank Mario Biagioli, Albert DiCanzio,

Annibale Fantoli, Owen Gingerich, Ron Naylor, Mauro Pesce, Jürgen Renn, Michael Segre, and Peter Slezak.

Furthermore, I have benefited greatly from many previous works on the trial of Galileo, and my notes contain explicit and specific citations. However, these references do not begin to give full credit to these authors, since I have often adapted without acknowledgment the information they provide. Thus I take this opportunity to say that I am generally indebted not only to Antonio Favaro (1890–1909), but also to Antonio Beltrán Marí (2006), Francesco Beretta (1998; 1999; 2005), Richard Blackwell (1991; 2006), Massimo Bucciantini (1995), Massimo Bucciantini and Michele Camerota (2009), Michele Camerota (2004), Alfredo Damanti (2010), Annibale Fantoli (2003), Pierre-Noël Mayaud (1997; 2005), Thomas Mayer (2012; 2013), Sergio Pagano (2009), Eileen Reeves and Albert van Helden (2010), and Jules Speller (2008).

On a different level, I am grateful to Brian Rak, editorial director at Hackett Publishing Company. His assistance has been not only administrative, but also inspirational.

Last but not least, I owe a special debt of gratitude to the University of Nevada, Las Vegas; its Department of Philosophy; its chairman, David Beisecker; and my colleagues Ian Dove, David Forman, Todd Jones, Bill Ramsey, Paul Schollmeier, and James Woodbridge. They have continued to provide institutional and moral support, even after I decided to retire from formal teaching in order to work full time on research, scholarship, and writing.

Introduction

This Introduction provides a guide to the appreciation of the documents translated and collected in this book. These are the most important documents that are essential to form an intelligent opinion regarding the trial of Galileo, based on some knowledge, understanding, and assessment of relevant facts, problems, and issues. Accordingly, this Introduction provides, in part, a synoptic overview (§0.5–§0.7) of the series of developments that began with Galileo's telescopic astronomical discoveries in 1609–1610; reached a temporary resolution in 1615–1616; climaxed with his trial and condemnation as a heretic by the Inquisition in 1632–1633; and acquired a definite character with the Church's implementation of his sentence during the rest of his life, 1633–1642. However, in order to make these developments understandable, that synoptic overview is preceded by a historical contextualization (§0.3–§0.4) sketching two things: the controversy engendered by Nicolaus Copernicus's hypothesis of a moving earth, and Galileo's reassessment of the Copernican hypothesis in light of his own telescopic discoveries. But even before sketching such a historical contextualization, it is useful to begin with a methodological discussion (§0.1–§0.2) outlining the balanced approach which is necessary to avoid common pitfalls and derive sound lessons, and which involves awareness and mastery of a number of conceptual distinctions.

§0.1 Anti-clerical vs. Anti-Galilean Myths and Other Distinctions

The most common view of the trial of Galileo is that it epitomizes the conflict between enlightened science and obscurantist religion. One version of this view is found inscribed in a public monument in Rome near Villa Medici, the palace where Galileo resided on some of his visits to Rome, and where he was held under house arrest for about a week after the 1633 sentence. The inscription reads: "it was here that Galileo was kept prisoner by the Holy Office, being guilty of having seen that the earth moves around the sun." The historical and cultural importance of this minor tourist attraction is that it expresses one of the most common myths widely held about the trial of Galileo, including several elements: that he "saw" the earth's motion (an observation still impossible to make even in the twenty-first century); that he was "imprisoned" by the Inquisition (whereas he was actually held under house arrest); and that his crime was to have discovered the truth. And since to condemn someone for this reason can result only from ignorance, prejudice, and narrow-mindedness, this is also the myth that alleges the incompatibility between science and religion.

The fact that I have described this critical interpretation of the trial as a myth reveals part of my attitude: I believe that such a thesis is erroneous, misleading, and simplistic. However, this myth is very widespread. For example, various formulations of the myth have been advanced not only by relatively injudicious writers who have recently been discredited (e.g., John W. Draper and Andrew D. White), but also by such classics and cultural icons as Voltaire, Albert Einstein, Bertrand Russell, and Karl Popper.[1]

One reason for identifying this first anti-clerical myth about the trial of Galileo is that it may be usefully contrasted to a second myth at the opposite extreme. It seems that some found it appropriate to fight an unpleasant myth by constructing another. The anti-Galilean myth maintains that Galileo deserved condemnation because he violated not only various ecclesiastical norms, but also various rules of scientific methodology and logical reasoning; he is thus portrayed as a master of cunning and knavery, and it is difficult to find a misdeed of which the proponents of this myth have not accused him. The history of this myth too has its own fascination, and it too includes illustrious names, such as French physicist, philosopher, and historian Pierre Duhem, German playwright Bertolt Brecht, Hungarian intellectual Arthur Koestler, and Austrian-American philosopher Paul Feyerabend.[2]

These two opposite myths are useful reference points for orienting oneself in the study of the controversy, since it is impossible to evaluate the trial adequately unless one admits that both of these accounts are mythological and thus rejects both. However, avoiding them is easier said than done. For example, one cannot simply follow a mechanical approach of mediating a compromise by dividing in half the difference that separates them. A helpful way of proceeding is to read the relevant texts and documents with care and with an awareness of a number of crucial conceptual distinctions.

One of the most important of these distinctions is that the trial of Galileo involved questions about both the truth of nature and the nature of truth, to use Owen Gingerich's (1982) eloquent expression. That is, the controversy was at least two-sided: it involved partly *scientific issues* about physical facts, natural phenomena, and astronomical and cosmological matters; and it also involved *methodological* and *epistemological questions* about what truth is and the proper way to search for it, and about what knowledge is and how to acquire it.

---

1. For more details and appropriate references, see Finocchiaro 2005, 115–19, 261; 2009; 2010, 293; 2014, 311–14.
2. For further details and references, see Finocchiaro 2005, 266–69, 295–317; 2010, xxxi–xxxvii, 200–301; 2014, 241–58, 316–27.

The overarching scientific issue was whether the earth stands still at the center of the universe, with all heavenly bodies revolving around it, or whether the earth is itself a heavenly body that rotates on its axis every day and revolves around the sun once a year. There were several distinct but interrelated questions here. One was whether the whole universe revolves daily from east to west around a motionless earth, or the earth rotates daily on its axis in the opposite direction (west to east); this was the problem of whether the so-called *diurnal motion* belongs to the earth or to the rest of the universe. Another question was whether the sun revolves yearly from west to east around the earth, or the earth revolves in the same way around the sun; this was the issue of whether the so-called *annual motion* belongs to the sun or to the earth. Another aspect of the controversy was whether the center of the universe, or at least the center of the revolutions of the planets, is the earth or the sun. And there was also the problem of whether the universe is divided into two very different regions, containing bodies made of different elements, having different properties, and moving and behaving in different ways: the terrestrial or sublunary part where the earth, including water and air, are located; and the celestial, heavenly, or superlunary region, beginning at the moon and extending beyond to include the sun, planets, and fixed stars.

The traditional view may be labeled *geostatic*, insofar as it claims the earth to be motionless; or *geocentric*, insofar as it locates the earth at the center of the universe; or *Ptolemaic*, insofar as in the second century A.D. the Greek astronomer Ptolemy had elaborated it in sufficient detail to make it a workable theoretical system; or *Aristotelian*, insofar as it corresponded to the worldview advanced in the fourth century B.C. by the Greek philosopher Aristotle, whose ideas in a wide variety of fields had become predominant in the sixteenth century. The other view may be called either *geokinetic*, insofar as it holds the earth to be in motion; or *heliocentric*, insofar as it places the sun at the center; or *Copernican*, named after the Polish astronomer Nicolaus Copernicus (1473–1543), who in the first half of the sixteenth century elaborated its details into a workable theoretical system; or *Pythagorean*, named after the ancient Greek pre-Socratic Pythagoras, who was one of the earliest thinkers (sixth century B.C.) to advance the idea in a general way. We may thus say that the scientific issue was essentially whether the geostatic or the geokinetic theory is true, or at least whether one or the other is more likely to be true.

The epistemological and methodological issues were several. First, there was the question of whether or not physical truth has to be directly observable, or whether any significant phenomenon (e.g., the earth's motion) can be true even though our senses cannot detect it, but can detect only its effects; here, one should remember that even today the earth's motion cannot be seen directly by an observer on earth. Second, there was the question of whether artificial instruments like the telescope have any legitimate role in the search for truth, or whether the proper way to proceed is to use only the natural senses; here, it should be mentioned that the telescope was the first artificial instrument ever used to learn novel scientific or philosophical truths about the world (as distinct from instruments like the compass that yield practical information). A third issue of this sort involved the question of the role of the Bible in scientific inquiry, whether its assertions about natural phenomena have any authority, or whether the search for truth about nature ought to be conducted completely independently of the claims contained in the Bible (cf. §1–§2); in this regard, it should be noted that this was not only a methodological or epistemological issue, but also a theological or hermeneutical one, and that this was the paramount issue in the trial, since it was widely believed that the new geokinetic theory contradicted the Bible. Fourth, there was the question of the nature of hypotheses and their role in the search for truth: whether they are merely instruments for mathematical calculation and observational prediction that can be only more or less convenient but neither true nor false, or whether they are assumptions about physical reality that are more or less probable and potentially true or false but not yet known with certainty (cf. §3–§4); here, this problem stemmed from the fact that even the anti-Copernicans admitted that one could explain the motion of the heavenly bodies by means of the hypothesis of the earth's motion, but they took this as a sign of its instrumental convenience and not of its truth, potential truth, or probable truth. Let us call these four central issues, respectively, the problems of the observability of truth, the legitimacy of artificial instruments, the scientific authority of the Bible, and the role of hypotheses (or the problem of instrumentalism vs. realism).

For the second needed conceptual clarification, one must distinguish between *factual correctness* and *rational correctness*, that is, between being right about the truth of the matter and having the right reasons for believing the truth. Suppose we begin by asking who was right about the scientific issue. It is obvious that Galileo was right and his opponents wrong, since he preferred the geokinetic to the geostatic view, and today we know for a fact that the earth does move and is not standing still at the center of the universe. However, it is equally clear that his being right about this does not *necessarily* mean that his motivating reasons were correct, since it is conceivable that although he might have chanced to hit upon the truth, his supporting arguments may have been unsatisfactory. Hence, the evaluation of his arguments is a separate issue.

I am not saying that the various proponents of the anti-Galilean accounts are right when they try to show that his arguments left much to be desired, ranging from inconclusive to weak to fallacious to sophistical. In fact, this evaluation is in my opinion untenable.[3] Rather, I am saying that Galileo's

---

3. For details, see Finocchiaro 1980, 180–255, 343–412; 2010, 229–50, 277–90; 2014, 243–58.

critics have raised a distinct and important issue *about* Galileo's trial—namely, whether or not, or to what extent, his *reasoning* was correct.

The next distinction that must be appreciated is also easy when stated in general terms but extremely difficult to apply in practice. It is that *essential correctness* must not be equated with either *total correctness* or *perfect conclusiveness*. Applied to our case, this means that even if Galileo's arguments were essentially correct, as I would hold, the possibility must be allowed that the reasoning of his opponents was neither worthless, nor irrelevant, nor completely unsound.[4] This point is a consequence of the fact that we are dealing with non-apodictic arguments which are not completely conclusive, but rather susceptible of degrees of rational correctness, and so it is entirely conceivable that there should sometimes be good arguments in support of opposite sides, as well as that the arguments for one side should sometimes be better than those for the opposite, without the latter being worthless. I believe this is the case for the trial of Galileo, though it is something the anti-clerical critics do not seem to be able to understand. The proper antidote here is the study of the details of the relevant arguments.

To appreciate the next distinction, let us ask the whether Galileo or the Church was right in regard to the epistemological and methodological aspect of the controversy. Since such issues are normally more controversial than scientific ones, this is an area which some like to exploit by trying to argue that the Church's epistemological and philosophical insight was superior to Galileo's. The argument is usually made in the context of a frank and explicit admission that Galileo was unquestionably right on the scientific issue. Thus, these anti-Galilean critics often boast of displaying even-handedness and balanced judgment by contending that on the one hand Galileo was right from a scientific or factual point of view, but that on the other hand the Church was right from an epistemological or philosophical point of view.

However, such interpretations can be criticized for their exaggeration, one-sidedness, and superficiality in their analysis of the epistemological component of the affair.[5] For example, I have already mentioned that there were at least four epistemological issues in the affair, and I am very doubtful that they can all be reduced to one. Moreover, it cannot be denied that Galileo turned out to be right on at least *some* of the epistemological issues—for example, those pertaining to the legitimacy of artificial instruments and to the Bible lacking scientific authority. On this last point, it should be mentioned that it is now more than one hundred years since the Catholic Church officially adopted the Galilean principle that the Bible is an authority only in matters of faith and

---

4. Cf. Finocchiaro 1980, 114–15; 2010, 121–34; 2011; 2014, 259–64.
5. See Finocchiaro 1980, 103–66; 2005, 263–69, 338–58; 2010, 277–90; 2014, 243–80.

morals, and not in questions of natural science; this came about in 1893 with Pope Leo XIII's encyclical *Providentissimus Deus*. Furthermore, it seems to me that with the epistemological issues too one can apply the distinction between factual and rational correctness, and thus introduce the question of the rationale underlying the two conflicting positions. That is, it is useful to examine their respective arguments and try to determine which were the better ones, although this is more difficult here than in the case of the scientific arguments.

Finally, one must bear in mind that this episode was *not* merely an *intellectual* affair. Besides the scientific, epistemological, methodological, theological, and philosophical issues, and besides the arguments pro and con, there were legal, political, social, economic, personal, and psychological factors involved. To be sure, it would be a mistake to concentrate on these issues, or even to devote to them equal attention in comparison with the intellectual issues, for these latter constitute the heart of the episode, and so they must have priority. Nevertheless, it would be equally a mistake to neglect the more external factors altogether. To them I now turn.

§0.2 Non-intellectual Factors

Beginning with personal or psychological factors, it is easy to see that Galileo had a penchant for controversy, was a master of wit and sarcasm, and wrote with unsurpassed eloquence. Interacting with each other and with his scientific and philosophical virtues, these qualities contributed to his making many enemies and becoming involved in many other bitter disputes besides the main one that concerns us here.[6] Typically these disputes involved questions of priority of invention or discovery, and fundamental disagreements about the occurrence and interpretation of various natural phenomena.

It may be of some interest to give a brief list of these other major controversies: a successful lawsuit against another scholar for plagiarism in regard to Galileo's invention of a calculating device and in regard to its accompanying instructions; a dispute with his philosophy colleagues at the University of Padua, where he taught mathematics, about the exact location of the novas that became visible in the heavens in October 1604; a dispute with other philosophers in Florence in 1612 about why bodies float in water; a dispute with a German Jesuit astronomer named Christoph Scheiner about priority in the discovery of sunspots and about their proper interpretation, beginning in 1612 and lasting to the end of their lives; and a dispute with the Italian Jesuit

---

6. For more details on this aspect of Galileo's life, thought, and trial in particular, see Finocchiaro (1980, 3–26, 46–66; 2014, 281–302), Heilbron (2010; 2012), Koestler 1959.

astronomer Orazio Grassi (1590–1654) about the nature of comets, occasioned by the appearance of some of these phenomena in 1618. Considering all this and what it indicates about Galileo's personality, one may wonder how he managed to acquire and keep the many friends and admirers he did.

In regard to social and economic factors, it should be noted that Galileo was not wealthy. He had to earn his living, first as a university professor, and then under the patronage of the grand duke of Tuscany. During his university career, from 1589 to 1610, his economic condition was always precarious. His university salary was very modest, especially so given that he taught mathematics and thus received only a fraction of the remuneration given to a professor of philosophy. This only compounded other unlucky family circumstances, such as having to provide dowries for his sisters. Galileo was forced to supplement his salary by giving private lessons, by taking on boarders at his house, and by working in and managing a profitable workshop which built various devices, some of his own invention. His financial difficulties eased in the second half of his life when he attained the position of "philosopher and chief mathematician" to the grand duke of Tuscany. In this position he was constantly facing a different problem, however, stemming from the nature of patronage and his relationship to his patron: since the fame and accomplishments of an artist or scientist were meant to reflect on the magnificence of the patron, Galileo was in constant need to prove himself scientifically and philosophically, either by surpassing the original accomplishments that had earned him the position or by giving new evidence for that original worth.[7]

Let us now go on to the politics of Galileo's trial. Here we have first the political background of the Catholic Counter-Reformation.[8] Martin Luther had started the Protestant Reformation in 1517, and the Catholic Church had convened the Council of Trent in 1545–1563. So Galileo's troubles developed and climaxed during a time of violent struggle between Catholics and Protestants. Since he was a Catholic living in a Catholic country, it was also a period when the decisions of that council were being taken seriously and implemented and thus affected him directly. Aside from the question of papal authority, one main issue dividing the two camps was the interpretation of the Bible—both how specific passages were to be interpreted, and who was entitled to do the interpreting. The Protestants, of course, were inclined toward relatively novel and individualistic or pluralistic interpretations, whereas the Catholics were committed to relatively traditional interpretations by the appropriate authorities.

A more specific element of religious politics concerns the fact that the climax of the trial in 1632–1633 took place during the so-called Thirty Years

---

7. For useful accounts of this aspect of Galileo's life in general and the trial in particular, see Biagioli (1993; 2006), Finocchiaro 2013, and Westfall (1984; 1985; 1989).
8. Cf. Blackwell (1991; 2006), Feldhay 2000.

War (1618–1648) between Catholics and Protestants. At that particular juncture, Pope Urban VIII, who had earlier been an admirer and supporter of Galileo, was in an especially vulnerable position; thus not only could he not continue to protect Galileo, but he had to use Galileo as a scapegoat to reassert, exhibit, and test his authority and power. The problem stemmed from the fact that in 1632 the Catholic side led by the king of Spain and the Bohemian Holy Roman emperor, was disastrously losing the war to the Protestant side led by the king of Sweden, Gustavus Adolphus. Religion was not the only issue in the war, which was being fought also over dynastic rights and territorial disputes. In fact, ever since Urban's election in 1623, the pope's policy had been motivated primarily by political considerations, such as his wish to limit and balance the power of the Hapsburg dynasty, which ruled Spain and the Holy Roman Empire. Papal policy had also been motivated by personal interest—that is, cooperation with the French, whose support had been instrumental in his election, and who for nationalistic reasons also opposed the Hapsburg hegemony. However, in the wake of Gustavus Adolphus's spectacular victories, the Spanish and Imperial ambassadors were accusing Urban of having favored and helped the Protestant cause. They mentioned such things as his failure to send the kind of military and financial support which popes had usually provided on such occasions, and his refusal to declare the war a holy war. There were even suspicions of a more direct understanding with the Protestants. Thus, the pope's own religious credentials were being questioned, and there were rumors of convening a council to depose him.[9]

Then there was what may be called the Tuscan factor, which had at least two political aspects. One was that the Grand Duchy of Tuscany, whose ruler Galileo served, was closely allied with Spain, and so the pope's intransigence with him was in part a way of getting back at Spain. The other was related to the fact that many of the leading protagonists in Galileo's trial were Tuscan; for example, Cardinal Robert Bellarmine, the key figure in the earlier phase of the proceedings, and Pope Urban VIII (of the House of Barberini), the moving force of the later proceedings. Thus the entire episode has some of the flavor of a family squabble.

Finally, another political element involved the internal power struggle within the Church, on the part of various religious orders, primarily the Jesuits and the Dominicans, but to some extent also the Capuchins. Here, it is interesting to note that in the earlier phase of the trial in 1615–1616, Galileo seems to have been attacked by Dominicans and defended by Jesuits, whereas in the later phase in 1632-1633, it seems that the two religious orders had exchanged

---

9. On this topic, the classic sources are Ranke (1841, 2: 98–125, especially 116–19) and Pastor (1898–1953, 28: 271–321); for a more vivid account, see Redondi 1987, 227–32; see also Miller 2008 for a useful update.

roles. And it is important to appreciate the significance of such internal dissent; that is, the Church was far from being a monolithic entity.[10]

Just as the political background of the affair involved primarily matters of religious politics, so the legal background involved essentially questions of ecclesiastical, or "canon," law. In Catholic countries, the activities of intellectuals like Galileo were subject to the jurisdiction of the Congregation of the Index and the Congregation of the Holy Office, or the Inquisition. In the administration of the Catholic Church, a "congregation" is a committee of cardinals charged with some department of Church business.

The Congregation of the Index was instituted by Pope Pius V in 1571 with the purpose of book censorship. One of its main responsibilities was the compilation of a list of forbidden books (called *Index librorum prohibitorum*). This congregation was abolished by Pope Benedict XV in 1917, and thereafter book censorship was handled once again by the Congregation of the Holy Office, which had been in charge of the matter before 1571.

The Congregation of the Holy Office, in turn, had been instituted in 1542 by Pope Paul III with the purpose of defending and upholding Catholic faith and morals. One of its specific duties was to take over the suppression of heresies and heretics, which had been handled by the medieval Inquisition; hence, from that time onward, the "Holy Office" and the "Inquisition" became practically synonymous. In 1965, at the Second Vatican Council, its name was officially changed to Congregation for the Doctrine of the Faith.

At the time of Galileo, the Inquisition or Holy Office had a complex bureaucracy; the notion of heresy had been given something of a legal definition; and inquisitorial procedures had been more or less codified. Let us examine some of the most relevant details.[11]

The Inquisition was the most important and authoritative congregation in the Church. This was reflected partly in the fact that it was the only congregation whose head (called "prefect") was the pope himself. Moreover, its membership consisted of about ten cardinal-inquisitors, which made it the largest congregation. Furthermore, its powers were greater than the powers of any other congregation, in the sense that it was not only the supreme judicial tribunal adjudicating particular cases, but also a legislative body whose decisions could enact new laws or change previous ones. Although it usually

---

10. Cf. Feldhay 1995, Mayer (2012, 3), Segre (1991, 30), and Speller 2008.

11. The following account is based primarily on Masini 1621; but see also Eymericus 1578/1973 and Scaglia 1616?/1986. For recent accounts of this aspect of Galileo's trial, see Beretta (1998; 1999; 2005a; 2005b; 2005c), Mayer (2012; 2013), Pagano 2009, and Speller 2008; for an instructive comparison and contrast of Galileo's trial with other famous Inquisition trials, e.g., that of Giordano Bruno (1548–1600), see Finocchiaro 2002; for an analysis of a particularly revealing special topic (torture), see Finocchiaro 2009.

followed past practice and precedent and various explicitly formulated rules, it was not bound by them.

The Inquisition's bureaucracy was correspondingly numerous and complex. Like most other congregations, it had a secretary, whose position was usually filled by the most senior member of the committee, and whose task was to handle correspondence. However, unlike other congregations, it had a professional staff: the commissary, who played the role of an executive secretary; the assessor, who was the chief legal officer; the prosecutor; and the notary, who was in charge of record keeping. Each of these had an assistant. Then there were the consultants, who subdivided into two groups: legal experts and theologians. Finally, the Inquisition had offices in all major cities, each headed by a "provincial" inquisitor.

Although the Inquisition dealt with other offenses such as witchcraft, it was primarily interested in two main categories of crimes: formal heresy and suspicion of heresy. Here, the term *suspicion* did not have the modern legal connotation pertaining to allegation and contrasting it to proof. One difference between formal heresy and suspicion of heresy was the seriousness of the offense. For example, a standard Inquisition manual of the time stated that "heretics are those who say, teach, preach, or write things against the Holy Scripture; against the articles of the Holy Faith;...against the decrees of the Sacred Councils and the determinations made by the Supreme Pontiffs;...those who reject the Holy Faith and become Moslems, Jews, or members of other sects, and who praise their practices and live in accordance with them..." (Masini 1621, 16–17). The same manual stated that "suspects of heresy are those who occasionally utter propositions that offend the listeners...those who keep, write, read, or give others to read books forbidden in the *Index* and in other particular Decrees;...those who receive the holy orders even though they have a wife, or who take another wife even though they are already married;...those who listen, even once, to sermons by heretics..." (Masini 1621, 17–18).

Another difference between formal heresy and suspicion of heresy was whether or not the culprit, having confessed the incriminating facts, admitted having an evil intention (Masini 1621, 166–67). Furthermore, within the major category of suspicion of heresy, two main subcategories were distinguished: vehement suspicion of heresy and slight suspicion of heresy; their difference depended on the seriousness of the criminal act (Masini 1621, 188). Thus, in effect there were three main types of religious crimes, in descending order of seriousness: formal heresy, vehement suspicion of heresy, and slight suspicion of heresy.

In regard to procedure, there were two ways in which legal proceedings could begin: either by the initiative of an inquisitor, based on publicly available knowledge or publicly expressed opinion; or in response to a complaint filed by some third party, who was required to make a declaration of the purity of his motivation and to give a deposition. Then there were specific rules about the interrogation of defendants and witnesses; how injunctions and decrees were to be worded; how, when, and why interrogation by torture was to be used; and the various kinds of judicial sentences and defendant's abjurations with which to conclude the proceedings.

To summarize, a balanced approach to the study of Galileo's trial must avoid the two opposite extremes exemplified by the anti-Galilean and anti-clerical myths. There is no easy way of doing this, but it may help to distinguish scientific from epistemological (or methodological) issues, factual correctness from rational correctness, essential correctness from total correctness, the several epistemological issues from each other, intellectual from external factors, and the several external factors from each other (personal-psychological, social, economic, political, and legal). However, these distinct entities are also interrelated, so the point is not to deny their interaction, but to make sure they are not confused with one another. With these methodological tips in mind, we are now ready to sketch the promised historical contextualization (§0.3–§0.4) that will help us understand the synoptic overview (§0.5–§0.7) of the trial itself.

§0.3 The Copernican Controversy

In 1543, Copernicus published his epoch-making book *On the Revolutions of the Heavenly Spheres*. In it, he updated an idea originally advanced by the Pythagoreans and Aristarchus in ancient Greece, but almost universally rejected: the earth moves by rotating on its own axis daily and revolving around the sun yearly. This contradicted the traditional belief that the earth was standing still at the center of the universe, with all heavenly bodies revolving around it. In its essentials, this geokinetic idea turned out to be true, as we know today beyond any reasonable doubt, after five centuries of accumulating evidence. At the time, however, the situation was very different (cf. Finocchiaro 2010, 21–36).

Copernicus's accomplishment was a *new argument* supporting an *old idea:* he demonstrated in quantitative detail that the known facts about the motions of the heavenly bodies could be explained more simply and coherently if the sun rather than the earth is assumed to be motionless at the center, and the earth is taken to be the third planet circling the sun. For example, from the viewpoint of simplicity, there are thousands fewer moving parts in the Copernican system than in the geostatic system, since the apparent daily westward motion of all heavenly bodies around the earth is explained by the earth's daily eastward axial rotation, and thus there is only one body rotating daily, not thousands. Regarding explanatory coherence, this concept means the ability to explain many details of the observed phenomena by means of one's basic principles, without adding *ad hoc* assumptions. Copernicus could thus coherently explain the periodic changes in the brightness and direction of motion of the planets, whereas the geostatic explanations of these details were improvised piecemeal.

However, Copernicus's argument was a *hypothetical* one. That is, it was based on the claim that *if* the earth were in motion *then* the observed phenomena would result; but from this it does not follow necessarily that the earth is in motion. This claim does provide a reason for preferring the geokinetic idea, but it is not a decisive reason. It would be decisive only in the absence of contrary reasons. In short, one has to look at counterarguments, and there were many.

Some counterarguments were mechanical, namely based on physics—the science of motion. For example, according to traditional Aristotelian physics, if the earth moved then terrestrial bodies would have to move in ways that do not correspond to how they are known (and easily observed) to move: freely falling bodies could not fall vertically, but would be left behind slanting westward; westward gunshots would range farther than eastward ones, instead of ranging equally; and loose bodies not firmly attached to the ground would fly off toward the sky due to centrifugal force. There is no way of escaping these mechanical consequences unless one rejects Aristotelian physics. To reject it effectively, one must put something else in its place. This in turn involves building a new physics—something easier said than done. In short, Copernicus's astronomy contradicted the physics of the time; the motion of the earth seemed to be a physical impossibility.

A moving earth was also considered to be a philosophical absurdity. For Copernicus did not claim that he could either feel, see, or otherwise perceive the earth's motion. Like everyone else, his senses (eyes and kinesthetic awareness) told him that the earth is at rest. Thus, some people objected that if his hypothesis were true, then the human senses would be lying to us, and it was regarded as absurd that the senses should deceive us about such a basic phenomenon as the state of the terrestrial globe on which mankind lives. That is, the geokinetic hypothesis seemed to be in flat contradiction with direct sense-experience, and so to violate the fundamental epistemological principle claiming that under normal conditions the senses provide us with an access to reality.

The Copernican theory also faced empirical difficulties in astronomy. That is, it had observational consequences regarding the heavenly bodies that were not in fact observed (until the invention of the telescope). For example, it implied that the earth (being a planet) should share various physical properties with the other planets; that the planet Venus should show periodic phases similar to those of the moon; that the planet Mars should show periodic changes in apparent size and brightness of a factor of about sixty; and that the fixed stars should exhibit an annual shift in apparent position.

Finally, the geokinetic hypothesis faced religious or theological difficulties. One objection was that the earth's motion contradicted many biblical passages, which state or imply that the earth stands still. For example, Joshua 10:12–13 speaks of the miracle of stopping the sun: "Then spake Joshua to the Lord in the day when the Lord delivered up the Amorites before the children of Israel, and he said in the sight of Israel, 'Sun, stand thou still upon Gibeon; and thou, Moon, in the valley of Ajalon'. And the sun stood still, and the moon staid, until the people had avenged themselves upon their enemies" (King James Version). Other anti-Copernican passages were Ecclesiastes 1:5 and Psalms 104:5.

In Catholic circles, this biblical objection was supplemented by one appealing to the consensus of Church Fathers—the saints, theologians, and churchmen who had played a formative role in the establishment of Christianity. The argument claimed that all Church Fathers were unanimous in interpreting relevant biblical passages in accordance with the geostatic view; therefore, the geostatic system is binding on all believers, and to claim otherwise is erroneous or heretical.

A third religious objection was more theologically-sounding, based on the belief in the omnipotence of God: since God is all-powerful, he could have created any one of a number of worlds, for example one in which the earth is motionless; therefore, regardless of how much evidence there is supporting the earth's motion, we can never assert that this must be so, for that would be to limit God's power to do otherwise. This was the favorite anti-Copernican argument of Pope Urban VIII.

Regarding the religious objections, it is important to note two things. On the one hand, they were only part of the opposition to Copernicanism,[12] since there were also the mechanical objections, the astronomical counterevidence, and the epistemological arguments. On the other hand, religious criticism of Copernicanism was immediate, indeed it even antedated the publication of the *Revolutions*; it did not have to wait for Galileo.[13]

Copernicus knew that his hypothesis faced such difficulties. He realized that his novel argument did not conclusively prove the earth's motion, and that there were many counterarguments of apparently greater strength. He was also aware of the religious objections. I believe these were the reasons why he delayed publication of his book until he was near death, although his motivation was complex and is not yet completely understood and continues to be the subject of serious research.

---

12. Here and elsewhere, the term *Copernicanism* should not be construed in the essentialist manner characteristic of all *isms*, but rather in a nominalist manner as equivalent to *Copernican theory;* this enables us to avoid the problem of the undesirable connotation of such terms, which has led some scholars (Westman 2011, 20) to altogether avoid the term *Copernicanism*.

13. See, e.g., Mayaud (2005, 3: 76, 84–87; 6: 134–38); Westman 2011, 195–97.

However, Copernicus's argument was so important that it could not be ignored, and various attempts were made to come to terms with it, to assimilate it, to amplify it, or to defend it.

§0.4 Galileo's Reassessment of Copernicanism

The most significant response to the Copernican controversy was Galileo's. He was born in Pisa in 1564, became professor of mathematics at the university there in 1589, and then taught at the University of Padua in 1592–1610.

During this period, Galileo researched primarily the nature of motion. He was critical of Aristotelian physics; favorably inclined toward the statics and mathematics of Archimedes (287–212 B.C.); and innovatingly experimental, insofar as he pioneered the procedure of actively intervening into and manipulating natural phenomena, combining empirical observation with quantitative mathematization and conceptual theorizing. Following this approach he formulated, justified, and systematized various mechanical principles: an approximation to the law of inertia; the composition of motion; the laws that in free fall the distance fallen increases as the square of the time elapsed and the velocity acquired is directly proportional to the time; and the parabolic path of projectiles. However, he did not publish these results during that period; indeed he did not publish a systematic account of them until 1638, in *Two New Sciences* (cf. Galilei 2008, 295–367).

A main reason for this delay was that in 1609 Galileo became actively involved in astronomy. He was already acquainted with Copernicanism and was appreciative of the fact that Copernicus had advanced a novel argument. Galileo also had intuited that the geokinetic theory was generally more consistent with his new physics than was the geostatic theory; in particular, he was attracted to Copernicanism because he felt the earth's motion could best explain why the tides occur. But he had not published or articulated this general intuition and this particular feeling. Moreover, he was acutely aware of the strength of the observational astronomical evidence against Copernicanism. Thus, until 1609 Galileo judged that the anti-Copernican arguments outweighed the pro-Copernican ones.

However, the telescopic discoveries led Galileo to a major reassessment. In 1609, he perfected the telescope to such an extent as to make it an astronomically useful instrument that could not be duplicated by others for some time. By its means he made several startling discoveries, which he published the following year in *The Sidereal Messenger* (Galilei 2008, 45–84): the moon's surface is full of mountains and valleys; a profusion of other stars exist besides those visible with the naked eye; the Milky Way and the nebulas are dense collections of large numbers of individual stars; and the planet Jupiter has four moons revolving around it at different distances and with different periods.

As a result, Galileo became a celebrity; resigned his professorship at Padua; was appointed "philosopher and chief mathematician" to the grand duke of Tuscany; and moved to Florence the same year. Soon thereafter, he also discovered the phases of Venus and sunspots; on the latter, in 1613, he published the *History and Demonstrations concerning Sunspots* (cf. Galilei 2008, 97–102).

Although most of these discoveries were made independently by others, no one understood their significance as well as Galileo. The reason for this was threefold. Methodologically, the telescope implied a revolution in astronomy, insofar as it was a new instrument for the gathering of a new kind of data transcending the previous reliance on naked-eye observation. Substantively, those discoveries strengthened the case for Copernicanism by refuting almost all empirical astronomical objections and providing new supporting observational evidence. Finally, this reinforcement was not equivalent to settling the issue because there was still some astronomical counterevidence (mainly, the lack of annual stellar parallax); because the mechanical objections had not yet been answered and the physics of a moving earth had not yet been explicitly articulated, although it was implicit in the research he had already accomplished; and because the theological objections had not yet been refuted. Thus, Galileo conceived a work that would discuss all aspects of the question. But this synthesis of Galileo's astronomy, physics, and methodology was not published until 1632, in the *Dialogue on the Two Chief World Systems, Ptolemaic and Copernican* (Galilei 1997).

This delay was due to the fact that the theological aspect of the question got Galileo into trouble with the Church, acquiring a life of its own that drastically changed his life. These troubles make up what may be called the trial of Galileo: a sequence of developments that accelerated in 1610 with the publication of *The Sidereal Messenger*, reached a temporary resolution in 1616 with the Index's prohibition of the Copernican doctrine; climaxed in 1633 with the Inquisition's condemnation of Galileo; and acquired a permanent characterization with the implementation of his sentence during the rest of his life, 1633–1642. This series of developments may also be called the original Galileo affair, to distinguish it from the subsequent Galileo affair, which refers to the ongoing controversy about the original episode and whether his condemnation was right and whether it proves the incompatibility between science and religion. To these developments we now turn, aiming to provide, as previously mentioned, a synoptic overview.[14]

---

14. The account that follows is highly condensed, but these simplifications are meant to be first approximations that could be refined more precisely and deeply, not essentially altered; for such refinements and fuller documentation, see Finocchiaro (1989; 2005; 2010; 2014); cf. also Beltrán Marí 2006, Beretta (1998; 2005c), Bucciantini 1995, Fantoli (2003; 2012), Heilbron 2010, Mayaud 1997, Mayer 2012, Pagano 2009, Reeves and Helden 2010, and Speller 2008.

§0.5 Earlier Developments, 1610–1616

As already mentioned, scriptural criticism of Copernicus's theory of a moving earth immediately followed the diffusion of his work, and did not have to wait for Galileo's contributions for it to emerge. However, it was not until Galileo's telescopic discoveries in 1609–1613 that the criticism accelerated and the problem became a crisis.

In fact, three months after March 1610, when Galileo's *Sidereal Messenger* left the printing press, Martin Horky published *A Very Short Excursion against the Sidereal Messenger.* A few months after that, Ludovico delle Colombe compiled an essay "Against the Earth's Motion" that included theological objections; it circulated widely, but was left unpublished.

In May 1611, Galileo's views on lunar mountains were violently attacked at a lecture in Mantua attended by Cardinal Ferdinando Gonzaga and delivered by a Jesuit of the Parma College; Galileo found it deeply offensive and defended himself in a long letter to Christoph Grienberger, a Jesuit of the Roman College (Camerota 2004, 213). The same year, Francesco Sizzi published in Venice a book, entitled *Dianoia astronomica, optica, physica* (1611), objecting on scriptural grounds to Galileo's discovery of the satellites of Jupiter.

In 1612, Giulio Cesare Lagalla, professor of philosophy at the University of Rome, published in Venice a book *On the Phenomena in the Orb of the Moon,* disputing Galileo's lunar discoveries. By the summer of that year Galileo was worried enough that he asked Cardinal Carlo Conti for advice on whether Scripture really favors Aristotelian natural philosophy. Conti was an influential churchman in Rome and replied promptly in two thoughtful letters.[15] Galileo found his reply very reassuring. On 2 November of the same year, in a private conversation Dominican friar Niccolò Lorini attacked Galileo for being inclined to heresy by believing ideas, such as that the earth moves, which contradict Scripture; but on 5 November Lorini wrote Galileo a letter of apology.

In the fall of 1613, Ulisse Albergotti published a book, *Dialogue…in Which It Is Held…That the Moon Is Intrinsically Luminous…*, containing biblical criticism of Galileo's theories. And now we come to a crucial incident. In December 1613, the Grand Duchess Dowager Christina confronted one of Galileo's friends and followers named Benedetto Castelli, who had succeeded him in the chair of mathematics at the University of Pisa; she presented Castelli with the biblical objection to the motion of the earth. This was done in an informal, gracious, and friendly manner, and clearly as much

---

15. Conti to Galileo, 7 July and 18 August 1612, in Galilei 1890–1909, 11: 354–55, 376. Cf. Reeves and Helden 2010, 349–52; Finocchiaro 2010, 70; Mayer 2012, 41–43.

out of genuine curiosity as out of worry. Castelli answered in a way that satisfied both the duchess and Galileo, when Castelli informed him of the incident. However, Galileo felt the need to immediately write a very long letter (§1, below) to his former pupil, containing a detailed refutation of the biblical objection.

Although unpublished, Galileo's letter to Castelli began circulating widely, and copies were made. Some of these came into the hands of traditionalists, who soon passed to the counterattack. For example, in December 1614, at a church in Florence, a Dominican friar named Tommaso Caccini preached a Sunday sermon against mathematicians in general, and Galileo in particular, on the grounds that their beliefs and practices contradicted Scripture and were thus heretical.

Then, in February 1615, the already-mentioned Lorini sent a written complaint (§5) against Galileo to Cardinal Paolo Sfondrati, head of the Congregation of the Index and member of the Congregation of the Holy Office in Rome; Lorini enclosed Galileo's letter to Castelli as incriminating evidence. In March of the same year, Caccini made a personal appearance before the Roman Inquisition. In his deposition (§6), he charged Galileo with suspicion of heresy, based not only on the content of the letter to Castelli, but also on the *Sunspots* book (1613); and he mentioned some hearsay evidence of a general sort and of a more specific type, involving two individuals named Ferdinando Ximenes and Giannozzo Attavanti. The Roman Inquisition responded by ordering an examination of these two individuals and of the two mentioned writings.

In the meantime, Galileo was writing for advice and support to many friends and patrons who were either clergymen or had clerical connections. He had no way of knowing about the details of the Inquisition proceedings, which were a well-kept secret; but Caccini's sermon had been public, and also he was able to learn about Lorini's written complaint.

Galileo also wrote and started to circulate privately three long essays on the issues. One, the *Letter to the Grand Duchess Christina* (§2), dealt with the religious objections and was an elaboration of the letter to Castelli, which was thus expanded from eight to forty pages. Another essay, the "Considerations on the Copernican Opinion" (§4), began to sketch a way of answering the epistemological and philosophical objections, which Galileo had never done; the importance of such objections had recently been stressed in a famous letter by Cardinal Robert Bellarmine (§3) addressed to Carmelite friar Paolo Antonio Foscarini, who in January 1615 had published a book arguing that the earth's motion is compatible with Scripture. And the third essay, entitled "Discourse on the Tides,"[16] was an elementary discussion of the scientific

---

16. In Finocchiaro 1989, 119–33; Galilei 1890–1909, 5: 377–95.

issues, in the form of a new physical argument in support of the earth's motion based on its alleged ability to explain the existence of the tides and of the trade winds; this essay was an anticipation of what Galileo would later elaborate in the Fourth Day of the *Dialogue*.

In December 1615, after a long delay due to illness, Galileo went to Rome of his own initiative, to try to clear his name and prevent the condemnation of Copernicanism. He did succeed in the former, but not in the latter, undertaking.

In fact, the results of the Inquisition investigations were as follows. The consultant who examined the letter to Castelli reported favorably that in its essence its hermeneutical views did not deviate from Catholic doctrine.[17] The cross-examination of the two witnesses, Ximenes and Attavanti, exonerated Galileo from the hearsay evidence; his utterance of heresies was found to be baseless.[18] And the examination of his work on *Sunspots* failed to reveal any explicit assertion of the earth's motion or other presumably heretical assertion, if indeed the Inquisition officials examined this book. However, in the process, the status of Copernicanism had become enough of a problem that the Inquisition felt it necessary to consult its experts for a formal opinion.

On 24 February 1616, a committee of eleven consultants reported unanimously that Copernicanism was philosophically (that is, scientifically) false and theologically heretical or erroneous.[19] In a way, much of the tragedy of the Galileo affair stems from this opinion, which even Catholic apologists seldom if ever defend nowadays. Although indefensible, if one wants to understand how this opinion came about, one must recall all the traditional arguments against the earth's motion, based on empirical-astronomical, mechanical-physical, and epistemological-philosophical considerations, as well as the scriptural-theological ones. Moreover, one must view the judgment of heresy in the light of the two objections based on the words of the Bible and on the consensus of the Church Fathers; in the light of the traditional hierarchy of disciplines, which made theology the queen of the sciences, and which had been reaffirmed at the Fifth Lateran Council in 1513; and in the light of the Catholic Counter Reformation rejection of new and individualistic interpretations of the Bible. However, the Inquisition must have had some misgivings about the opinion of the committee of eleven consultants, for it issued no formal condemnation. Instead two milder consequences followed.

First, the Inquisition decided (§7) to give Galileo a private warning to stop defending and to abandon his geokinetic views; and if he did not agree, to issue him a formal injunction not to discuss the topic in any way

---

17. Finocchiaro 1989, 135–36; Galilei 1890–1909, 19: 305.
18. Finocchiaro 1989, 141–46; Galilei 1890–1909, 19: 316–20.
19. Finocchiaro 1989, 146–47; Galilei 1890–1909, 19: 320–21.

whatever. The warning was conveyed to Galileo by Cardinal Bellarmine, the most influential and highly respected theologian and churchman of the time, with whom Galileo was on very good terms, despite their philosophical and scientific differences. The exact content, form, and circumstances of this warning are not completely known, but they are extremely complex and a subject of great controversy. Moreover, as we shall see later, the occurrence and propriety of the later Inquisition proceedings in 1633 hinge on the nature of this warning. For now let us simply note that Bellarmine reported back to the Inquisition (§9) that he had warned Galileo to abandon his defense of and belief in the geokinetic thesis, and that Galileo had promised to obey.

The other development was a public decree (§10) issued by the Congregation of the Index on 5 March 1616, containing four main points. First, it stated that the doctrine of the earth's motion was false, contrary to the Bible, and a threat to Catholicism. Second, it condemned and completely prohibited Foscarini's book, which had tried to show that the earth's motion is compatible with Scripture. Third, it suspended circulation of Copernicus's book, pending correction and revision; these corrections were eventually issued in 1620, their gist being to delete or modify about a dozen passages containing religious references or language indicating Copernicus's realist interpretation of the earth's motion.[20] Fourth, the decree ordered analogous censures for analogous books. Galileo was not mentioned at all.

It should be noted that this was a decree issued by the Index, and not by the Holy Office or Inquisition; hence, although Catholics were still obliged to obey the decree, it did not carry the weight and generality of pronouncements which define the Catholic faith, just as even Inquisition decrees would not carry the authority of official papal decrees *ex cathedra* or decrees issued by ecumenical councils, such as the Council of Trent. Moreover, the actual wording in the decree was vague and unclear, which is a sign of its having been some kind of compromise, and the exact reason or the exact offensive features of the prohibited books were not spelled out; thus, the declaration that analogous works were analogously prohibited was too vague and liable to great abuse. Finally, one was left in the dark concerning what type of *discussion* of Copernicanism was indeed allowed.

In view of the confusing message in the Index's decree, and in view of the even more confusing circumstances of Bellarmine's private warning to Galileo (which I will discuss later), it is easy to sympathize with Galileo's next two moves before he left Rome to return home to Florence. He obtained an audience with Pope Paul V; and in a letter to the Tuscan secretary of state, Galileo reported that he had been warmly received and reassured, during

---

20. Finocchiaro 1989, 200–202; Galilei 1890–1909, 19: 400–401. Cf. Bucciantini 1995; Finocchiaro 2005, 20–25.

three-quarters of an hour with the pontiff.[21] Moreover, at this time Galileo
began receiving letters from friends in Venice and Pisa saying that there were
rumors in those cities to the effect that he had been put on trial, condemned,
forced to recant, and given appropriate penalties by the Inquisition. Having
shown these letters to Cardinal Bellarmine, Galileo was able to convince him
to write a brief and clear statement of what had happened and how Galileo
was affected. Thus in a document (§11) half a page long, the most authoritative churchman of his time declared the following: Galileo had been neither
tried nor otherwise condemned, but rather he had been personally notified
of the Index's decree, and of the fact that in view of this decree the geokinetic thesis could be neither held nor defended. With this certificate in his
possession, Galileo left Rome soon thereafter.

§0.6 Later Developments, 1616–1633

There is no question that these prohibitions of the Copernican doctrine had
a chilling effect on Catholics in general and Galileo in particular. In a sense,
they made official and explicit the illiberal and intolerant climate of opinion
which many had already sensed and experienced in the Rome of Pope Paul
V, and which is eloquently described in the report (§12) by Tuscan ambassador Piero Guicciardini to Grand Duke Cosimo II. Even persons and insti-
tutions that were independent-minded, such as the Republic of Venice and
its official theologian Fra Paolo Sarpi, had to find ways of accommodating
themselves to the anti-Copernican decree; a good example of this is Sarpi's
legal opinion to the doge (§14).[22]

As we have seen, neither Galileo nor his works were mentioned by name
in the anti-Copernican decree, a point he made sure to stress in his own report
to the Tuscan secretary of state (§13). Now, although this report was under-
standably silent about the personal warning he had received, on the basis of
Bellarmine's certificate Galileo was clear in his own mind that he had been at
least prohibited to advocate Copernicanism. Thus, it is not surprising that for
the next several years he refrained from defending or explicitly discussing the
geokinetic theory. Even the publication of the corrections to Copernicus's
book in 1620, which gave one a better idea of what was allowed and what
not, did not motivate him to resume the earlier struggle. The death of both
Bellarmine and Pope Paul V in 1621, and the election of Pope Gregory XV
did result in some encouragement, for example when Galileo was consulted

---

21. Finocchiaro 1989, 151–53; Galilei 1890–1909, 12: 247–49.
22. The responses were, of course, different among Protestants, such as Kepler; cf.
Bucciantini 1995, 99–116.

about astronomical matters by the cardinal nephew and Vatican secretary of state;[23] but those developments were not enough for a significant change.

On the other hand, it should not be surprising that Galileo too found his own way of assimilating the anti-Copernican prohibitions. For example, he did discuss Copernicanism implicitly and indirectly in the context of a controversy about the nature of comets, that is, in *The Assayer* (1623).[24] But this was a very small step, and there is no doubt that he was constantly searching for a better opportunity. This finally came in 1623, when Cardinal Maffeo Barberini was elected Pope Urban VIII.

Urban was a well-educated Florentine, and in 1616 he had been instrumental in preventing the direct condemnation of Galileo and the formal condemnation of Copernicanism as a heresy (cf. §30). He was also a great admirer of Galileo, and in 1620 he had even written a poem in praise of Galileo. He now employed as personal secretary one of Galileo's closest acquaintances, Giovanni Ciampoli. Further, at about this time, Galileo's *Assayer* was being published in Rome by the Lincean Academy, and so it was decided to dedicate the book to the new pope. Urban appreciated the gesture and liked the book very much. Finally, as soon as circumstances allowed, in the spring of 1624, Galileo went to Rome to pay his respects to the pontiff; he stayed six weeks and was warmly received by Church officials in general and the pope in particular, who granted him weekly audiences.

The details of the conversation during these six audiences are not known. There is evidence, however, that Urban VIII did not think Copernicanism to be a heresy, or to have been declared a heresy by the Church in 1616. He interpreted the Index's decree to mean that the earth's motion was a rash or dangerous doctrine whose study and discussion required special care and vigilance. He thought the theory could never be proved to be necessarily true, and here it is interesting to mention his favorite argument for this skepticism, namely the divine-omnipotence objection. This argument, together with his interpretation of the decree of 1616, must have reinforced his liberal inclination that, as long as one exercised the proper care, there was nothing wrong with the hypothetical discussion of Copernicanism; that is, with treating the earth's motion as a "hypothesis": studying its consequences, its value for understanding and explaining physical reality, and its utility for making astronomical calculations and predictions.

At any rate, Galileo must have gotten some such impression during his six conversations with Urban, for upon his return to Florence he began working on a book. This was in part the work on the system of the world which he had

---

23. Ludovisi to Galileo, 22 November 1622, in Galilei 1890–1909, 13: 100–101; cf. Beltrán Marí 2006, 381–87.
24. For the indirectly Copernican aspects of *The Assayer,* see Beltrán Marí 2006, 369–81; Biagioli 1993, 267–311; Camerota 2004, 363–98; Speller 2008, 111–23.

conceived at the time of his first telescopic discoveries, but it now acquired a new form and new dimensions in view of all that he had learned and experienced since. His first step was to write and circulate privately a lengthy reply to the anti-Copernican essay written in 1616 by Francesco Ingoli. This Galilean "Reply to Ingoli,"[25] as well as his earlier "Discourse on the Tides," were incorporated into the new book. After a number of delays (§15–§16) in its writing, licensing, and printing, the work was finally published in Florence in February 1632, with the title *Dialogue on the Two Chief World Systems, Ptolemaic and Copernican.*

The author had done many things to avoid trouble, to ensure compliance with the many restrictions under which he was operating, and to satisfy the various censors who issued him permissions to print. To emphasize the "hypothetical" character of the discussion, he had originally entitled the book *Dialogue on the Tides* and structured it accordingly. That is, it was to begin with a statement of the problem of the cause of tides, and then it would introduce the earth's motion as a hypothetical cause of the phenomenon; this would lead to the problem of the earth's motion, and to a discussion of the arguments pro and con, as a way of assessing the merits of this hypothetical explanation of the tides. However, the book censors, interpreting and acting upon the pope's wishes, decided (§16) to make the book look like a vindication of the Index's decree of 1616. The book's preface, whose content must be regarded as originating primarily from the pope and the censors and only secondarily from Galileo, claimed that the work was being published to prove to non-Catholics that Catholics knew all the arguments about the scientific issues, and so their decision to believe in the geostatic theory was motivated by religious reasons and not by scientific ignorance. It went on to add that the scientific arguments seemed to favor the geokinetic theory, but that they were inconclusive, and thus the earth's motion remained a hypothesis.

Galileo also complied with the explicit request to end the book with a statement of the pope's favorite argument, namely the objection from divine omnipotence. Moreover, to make sure he would not be seen as holding or defending the geokinetic thesis (which he knew he had been forbidden to do), he did two things. He wrote the book in the form of a dialogue among three speakers: Simplicio, defending the geostatic side; Salviati, taking the Copernican view; and Sagredo, an uncommitted observer who listens to both sides and accepts the arguments that seem to survive critical scrutiny. And in many places throughout the book, usually at the end of a particular topic, the Copernican Salviati utters the qualification that the purpose of the discussion is information and enlightenment, and not to decide the issue, which is a task

---

25. Finocchiaro 1989, 154–97; Galilei 1890–1909, 6: 509–61. Cf. Bucciantini 1995; Buciantini and Camerota 2009, 163–88.

to be reserved for the proper authorities. Finally, it should be mentioned that Galileo obtained written permissions to print the book (§15–§16), first from the proper Church officials in Rome (when the plan was to publish the book there), and then from the proper officials in Florence (when an outbreak of the plague made it impossible to ship the manuscript between Florence and Rome).

The book was well-received in scientific circles. However, a number of rumors and complaints began emerging and circulating in Rome.

One complaint involved a document that had been found in the file of the Inquisition proceedings of 1615–1616. The document (§8) reads like a report of what took place when Cardinal Bellarmine, on orders from the Inquisition, gave Galileo the private warning to stop defending his geokinetic views. The cardinal had died in 1621, and so was no longer available to clarify the situation. The document (§8) states that in February 1616, at the same meeting with Bellarmine, the Inquisition's commissary had given Galileo the formal injunction to stop holding, defending, or teaching the earth's motion in any way whatever. That is, this document states that Galileo had been given a special injunction, above and beyond what bound Catholics in general: supposedly, he had been prohibited not only to hold or defend the earth's motion as a truth, but also to hold or defend the idea in any manner as well as to teach it in any manner; in short, he was prohibited to discuss the topic at all. Obviously, even a hypothetical discussion violates such a prohibition. The charge was then that the book was a clear violation of this special injunction, since whatever else the book did, and however else it might be described, it undeniably contained a discussion of the earth's motion.

To be sure, the document did not bear Galileo's signature, and it contradicted other genuine documents (§7, §9, §11), and so it was of questionable legal validity. Under different circumstances such a judicial technicality could have been taken seriously. However, too many other difficulties were being raised about the book (§17–§19).

One difficulty was that the work only paid lip service to the stipulation about a hypothetical discussion, which represented Urban's compromise; in fact, the book allegedly treated the earth's motion not as a hypothesis, but in a factual, nonconditional, and realistic manner. This was a more or less legitimate complaint on the part of the pope, but the truth of the matter is that the concept of hypothesis was ambiguous and had not been sufficiently clarified in that historical context. By hypothetical treatment, Urban meant a discussion that would treat the earth's motion merely as an instrument of prediction and calculation, rather than as a potentially true description of reality. On the other hand, Galileo took a hypothesis to be an assumption about physical reality, which accounts for what is known, and which may be true, though it has not yet been proved to be true.

Third, there was the problem that Galileo's book was in actuality a defense of the geokinetic theory. Despite the dialogue form, despite the repeated disclaimers that no assertion of Copernicanism was intended, despite the nonapodictic and nonconclusive character of the pro-Copernican arguments, and despite the presentation of the anti-Copernican and pro-geostatic arguments, it was readily apparent that the pro-geostatic arguments were being criticized and the pro-Copernican ones were being portrayed favorably. And this perception led some to claim that the book was arguing in favor of Copernicanism and hence was defending it.

There were also complaints involving alleged irregularities in the various permissions to print that Galileo obtained. There were substantive criticisms of various specific points discussed in the book. There were hurt feelings about some of his rhetorical excesses and biting sarcasm. There were malicious slanders suggesting that the book was in effect a personal caricature of the pope himself.

Although some of the complaints in the last miscellaneous group were easily cleared, the sheer number in the whole list and the seriousness of some of the charges were such that the pope might have been forced to take some action even under normal circumstances. But, as mentioned earlier, Urban VIII was himself in political trouble due to his behavior in the Thirty Years War. At that particular juncture the pope was in an especially vulnerable position, and thus not only could he not continue to protect Galileo, but he probably chose to use Galileo as a scapegoat to reassert his authority and power.

Thus, in the summer of 1632 sales of the book were stopped, unsold copies were confiscated, and a special commission was appointed to investigate the matter. The pope did not immediately send the case to the Inquisition, but he took the unusual step of appointing a special commission first. This three-member panel issued its report (§19) in September 1632, and it listed as areas of concern about the book all of the above-mentioned problems, with the exception of the malicious slanders. In view of the report, the pope felt he had no choice but to forward the case to the Inquisition. Or rather, this was the impression Urban wanted to convey and what he said to the Tuscan ambassador to Rome (§17); for the report can be read as leaving the question open. It is more likely that Urban was mostly manipulating the proceedings: he may have been trying to cover up his own permissiveness and complicity in the writing and publication of the *Dialogue;* or he may have been acting on his (questionable) perception that this book came close to formal heresy by its failure to treat hypothetically (instrumentalistically) of the earth's motion and to show the proper appreciation for divine omnipotence. So Galileo was summoned to Rome to stand trial.

The entire autumn was taken up by attempts on the part of Galileo and the Tuscan government to prevent the inevitable. The Tuscan government got

involved partly because of Galileo's position as "philosopher and chief mathematician" to the grand duke; partly because the book contained a dedication
to the grand duke; and partly because the grand duke had been instrumental
in getting the book finally printed in Florence. At first they tried to have the
trial moved from Rome to Florence. Then they asked that Galileo be sent
the charges in writing, and that he be allowed to respond in writing. As a last
resort, three physicians signed a medical certificate stating that Galileo was
too ill to travel. This was true, and here it should be added that he was sixty-
eight years old, and that there had been an outbreak of the plague for the past
two years, which meant that travelers from Tuscany to the Papal States were
subject to quarantine at the border. At the end of December the Inquisition
sent Galileo an ultimatum: if he did not come to Rome of his own accord,
they would send some officers to arrest him and bring him to Rome in chains.
On 20 January 1633, after making a last will and testament, Galileo began the
journey. When he arrived in Rome three weeks later, he was not arrested
or imprisoned by the Inquisition, but was allowed to lodge at the Tuscan
embassy (Palazzo Firenze), though he was ordered not to socialize and to keep
himself in seclusion until he was called for interrogations.[26]

These were slow in coming, as if the Inquisition wanted to use the tor-
ment of the uncertainty, suspense, and anxiety as part of the punishment to
be administered to the old man. This was very much in line with one reason
mentioned earlier by officials why Galileo had to make the journey to Rome,
despite his old age, ill health, and the epidemic of the plague; that is, he had
to do it as an advance partial punishment or penance, and if he did this the
inquisitors might take it into consideration when the time of the actual proceedings came.

The first interrogation was held on 12 April (§20). The questions did not
focus on Pope Urban's complaint about the book's failure to treat the earth's
motion hypothetically and to appreciate divine omnipotence, but rather on
the events of 1616. In answer to various questions, the defendant claimed the
following. He admitted having been given a warning by Cardinal Bellarmine
in February 1616, and described this as an oral warning that the geokinetic
theory could be neither held nor defended, but only discussed hypothetically.
He denied having received any special injunction not to discuss the earth's
motion in any way whatever, and he introduced Bellarmine's certificate (§11)
as supporting evidence. His third main claim was made in answer to the question why he had not obtained any permission to write the book in the first
place, and why he had not mentioned Bellarmine's warning when obtaining
permission to print it; these omissions had angered the pope and had made

---

26. For details about Galileo's non-imprisonment and whereabouts during the 1633
trial, see Finocchiaro 2009.

him feel deceived. Galileo answered that he had not done so because the book did not hold or defend the earth's motion, but rather showed that the arguments in its favor were not conclusive, and thus it did not violate Bellarmine's warning.

This was a very strong and practicable line of defense. In particular, Galileo's third point may be interpreted to suggest that the *Dialogue* was *discussing,* not defending, the earth's motion, insofar as it was a critical examination of the arguments on both sides (cf. §18).[27] Moreover, just as the special injunction was news to Galileo, so Bellarmine's certificate must have surprised and disoriented the Inquisition officials. Thus, it took another three weeks before they finally decided on the next step in the proceedings. In the meantime Galileo was detained at the headquarters of the Inquisition, but allowed to lodge in the prosecutor's apartment.

What the inquisitors finally decided was something very close to what might be called an out-of-court settlement involving a plea-bargaining agreement. That is, they would not press the most serious charge (of having violated the special injunction), nor the charge of having violated Urban's request for a hypothetical treatment of the earth's motion and an appreciation of divine omnipotence; but Galileo would have to plead guilty to the lesser charge of having inadvertently transgressed the warning not to defend Copernicanism, in regard to which his defense was the weakest; and to reward such a confession, they would show leniency toward such a lesser violation.

The deal was worked out as follows. The Inquisition asked three consultants to determine whether or not Galileo's *Dialogue* taught, defended, or held the geokinetic theory; in separate reports all three concluded that the book clearly taught and defended the doctrine, and came close to holding it.[28] Then the Inquisition's commissary talked privately with Galileo to try to arrange the deal, and after lengthy discussions he succeeded (§21). Galileo requested and obtained a few days to think of a dignified way of pleading guilty to the lesser charge.

On 30 April, the defendant appeared before the Inquisition for the second time, and signed a deposition stating the following (§22). Ever since the first hearing he had reflected about whether, without meaning to, he might have done anything wrong. It dawned on him to reread his book, which he had not done for the past three years since completing the manuscript. He was surprised by what he found, because the book did give the reader the impression that the author was defending the geokinetic theory, even though this had not been his intention. To explain how this could have happened, Galileo

---

27. For details and references on this issue, see Finocchiaro 2010, 242–43; 2011; 2014, 255–58, 322.
28. Finocchiaro 1989, 262–76; Galilei 1890–1909, 19: 348–60.

attributed it to vanity, literary flamboyance, and an excessive desire to appear clever by making the weaker side look stronger. He was deeply sorry for this transgression and ready to make amends.

After this deposition, Galileo was allowed to return to the Tuscan embassy. On 10 May, there was a third formal hearing (§23–§24) at which he presented his defense, including the original copy of Bellarmine's certificate; Galileo repeated his recent admission of some wrongdoing together with a denial of any malicious intent, and added a plea for clemency and pity. The trial might have ended here, but was not concluded for another six weeks.

Obviously the pope and the Inquisition cardinals would have to approve the final disposition of the case. Indeed, it was standard Inquisition procedure for an official (usually the assessor) to compile a summary of the proceedings for the benefit of the cardinal-inquisitors. So a report was written, summarizing the events from 1615 to Galileo's third deposition just completed.[29] Through a series of misrepresentations, this report left no doubt that Galileo had committed some criminal act; on the other hand, by various quotations from his confessions and pleas, the report made it clear that he was not obstinately incorrigible, but rather sorry and willing to submit. However, this did not resolve Urban's doubts about Galileo's intention. Thus, the pope decided (§25) that the defendant should be interrogated under the verbal threat of torture in order to determine his intention; furthermore, even if his intention was found to have been pure, he had to make an abjuration and was condemned to formal arrest at the pleasure of the Inquisition; and the *Dialogue* had to be banned.

Threat of torture and actual torture were, at the time, standard practices of the Inquisition, and indeed of almost all systems of criminal justice in the world (cf. Finocchiaro 2009). Nevertheless, such an interrogation, together with the abjuration, the arrest, and the book ban were not really in accordance with the spirit or the letter of the out-of-court plea-bargaining and agreement. Thus, Galileo felt betrayed and remained always bitter about this outcome.

On 21 June, Galileo was subjected to the interrogation under the formal verbal threat of torture (§26). The result was favorable, in the sense that, even under such a threat, Galileo denied any malicious intention, and showed his readiness to die rather than admit such intention.

The following day, at the convent of Santa Maria sopra Minerva in Rome, he was read the sentence and then recited the formal abjuration. The sentence (§27) found Galileo "vehemently suspected of heresy." As mentioned earlier, this referred to a specific category of religious crime—vehement suspicion of heresy—intermediate in seriousness between formal heresy and slight suspicion of heresy. In effect, Galileo was being convicted of the second most serious offense handled by the Inquisition. Two distinct allegedly heretical

---

29. Finocchiaro 1989, 281–86; Galilei 1890–1909, 19: 293–97.

views were mentioned: the astronomical and cosmological thesis that the earth rotates daily on its axis and circles the sun once a year; and the methodological and theological principle that one may believe and defend as probable a thesis contrary to the Bible.

The sentence also banned the *Dialogue*; condemned Galileo to indefinite imprisonment; gave him the religious penance of reciting the seven penitential psalms once a week for three years; and required him to recite a formal abjuration immediately after the reading of the sentence. The abjuration (§28), which was provided to him by the officials, happened to contain more than expressions of sorrow for past actions, promises about future ones, and the admission of guilt for having inadvertently violated Bellarmine's warning not to defend the earth's motion, which he had agreed upon since the second deposition. The text of the abjuration also forced Galileo to admit having received and thus violated the special injunction not to discuss the topic in any way whatever, which he had denied during the trial.

Another interesting detail about the sentence is that only seven out of the ten cardinal-inquisitors signed it. Two of the three who did not were Francesco Barberini, the pope's nephew and Vatican secretary of state, who was the most powerful man in Rome after the pope himself, and Gaspare Borgia, Spanish ambassador and leader of the Spanish party, who a year earlier had threatened the pope with impeachment for his behavior in the Thirty Years War. The explanation of the missing signatures became one of the many controversial issues of the subsequent Galileo affair: whether it reflects dissent or merely a poor attendance record by the absentees.[30]

§0.7 Final Incidents, 1633–1642

The Church's attitude and actions regarding Galileo's imprisonment turned out to be relatively benign (cf. §31). The following day (23 June), his prison sentence was commuted to house arrest at Villa Medici, a sumptuous palace in Rome owned by the grand duke of Tuscany. A week later, this was again commuted to house arrest in Siena, at the residence of the archbishop, who was a good friend of Galileo. He was made to feel so comfortable there that he resumed his work on the physics of motion which he had set aside for more than two decades; thus, he started working on the book which would become the *Two New Sciences* and be published in 1638. Indeed, he was treated with such respect and honor by the archbishop that in February 1634 an anonymous complaint was filed with the Inquisition, against Galileo and the archbishop, regarding such treatment.

---

30. Cf. Finocchiaro 2005, 369 n. 21; Mayer 2013, 39–40, 218–21.

However, the complaint had no effect because by then Galileo had been granted his wish to go back home. In fact, on 1 December, the Siena location had been commuted once again, now to house arrest at Galileo's own villa in Arcetri, near Florence. Later that month he moved to his Arcetri villa. After he became completely blind in December 1637, he was even allowed to reside at his small house in Florence for medical reasons, although under the same conditions of house arrest. But he apparently preferred the greater comfort and freedom of his villa, and so after about nine months in Florence, in January 1639 he moved back to Arcetri. He stayed there until his death in 1642.

In other ways, the Church's attitude and actions were harsher. For example, in the summer of 1633, all papal nuncios in Europe and all local inquisitors in Italy received copies of the sentence against Galileo and of his abjuration, together with orders to publicize them. Such publicity was unprecedented in the annals of the Inquisition and would never be repeated in subsequent inquisitorial practice. The orders were transmitted by means of a memorandum (§29) signed on 2 July by Cardinal Antonio Barberini, the pope's brother and Inquisition's secretary.

Moreover, various attempts were made to obtain a pardon, but all to no avail. Some of these petitions were made, naturally enough, by Galileo himself and by the Tuscan government. However, other pleas were made by the French ambassador to the Holy See, François Count de Noailles, and by Ladislaus IV, King of Poland.[31] The most eloquent and poignant plea for a pardon was made by Nicolas Claude Fabri de Peiresc, a Frenchman who was extremely well connected and was on friendly terms with the pope's family. He directed his plea (§32) to Cardinal Francesco Barberini. In December 1634, and then again in January 1635, he wrote to Barberini, who politely acknowledged receipt, but was vague and noncommittal about a pardon.

Such pleas were not only unsuccessful, but also may have backfired, in the sense that they seemed to harden the pope's and Inquisition's attitude. For example, as we learn from Galileo's letter to Diodati (§31), in the spring of 1634 Galileo was informed that no more pleas and petitions would be tolerated, on pain of his house arrest being commuted back to imprisonment in the Inquisition's jail.

The same letter also mentions the revealing detail that the 1633 trial may have been initiated or instigated by the Jesuits. This is a plausible possibility, in light of the bitter disputes Galileo had with some of them, with Scheiner over sunspots and with Grassi over comets. The Jesuits' possible involvement is also mentioned in the account of the trial compiled by Giovanfrancesco Buonamici (§30), and was echoed by René Descartes in his reflections on the

---

31. Galilei 1890-1909 (16: 171, 420–21, 458–59; 17: 26–27); cf. Finocchiaro 2005, 55–56, 69–70.

trial.[32] Although plausible, such a "conspiracy theory" cannot be taken at face value, and was to become an issue in the subsequent Galileo affair.

Besides refusing a pardon, the Church seemed to increase Galileo's punishment. As he mentioned in his letter to Peiresc (§33), the additional penalty was an alleged prohibition against publishing any of his works. Galileo was referring to something he had just learned from Fra Fulgenzio Micanzio, the official theologian of the Republic of Venice, an independent-minded Venetian, strong supporter of Galileo, and successor to Sarpi. Micanzio had offered to help Galileo publish in Venice the new work on physics which he had started writing in Siena. Although this did not deter the fearless Micanzio, he pointed out that publishing the *Two New Sciences* in Venice might cause Galileo unnecessary trouble; thus, the book was eventually published in Holland.

However, again, the complexity of the situation, and the nuanced character of the Church's attitude, should not be ignored. Thus, it is important to note that Galileo did not seem to suffer any harm from the Inquisition for publishing this book. Indeed, in January 1639, the book reached Rome's bookstores, and all available copies (about fifty) were quickly sold and everyone seemed to like it.

Nevertheless, the final incident that must serve here to end our story of Galileo's original trial[33] is an expression of ecclesiastic animosity against him. He died at Arcetri on 8 January 1642. The following day he was quietly buried at the church of Santa Croce in Florence, not in the family tomb within the church proper, but in a grave without decoration or inscription, located in an out-of-the-way room behind the sacristy and under the bell tower. There was considerable interest in Florence to build a sumptuous mausoleum for him in the same church; in fact, Galileo's friends quickly raised three thousand scudi (in pledges) from the Florentine intelligentsia and elites for the project. To be sure, Galileo's enemies raised the question of whether it was permissible in canon law to erect an honorary mausoleum for a man condemned of vehement suspicion of heresy; but a formal legal opinion was written, concluding that it was not illegal. At any rate, within days of Galileo's death, the Florentine nuncio informed Rome that Galileo was dead and that the grand duke was planning to build a mausoleum for him in the church of Santa Croce. However, as we can see from Niccolini's letter to Gondi (§34) of 25 January 1642, the pope and the Inquisition let the grand duke know that it would not be pious or proper to build a mausoleum for a condemned heretic like Galileo. The grand duke acquiesced, and it took a century before the mausoleum project was accomplished.

---

32. Galilei 1890–1909, 16: 56; Finocchiaro 2005, 44–45.
33. For the continuation of the story to our own day, see Finocchiaro 2005.

Glossary of Terms and Names

ad hominem. In the seventeenth century, this meant an argument designed to examine the correctness of a controversial view by showing that it implies consequences not acceptable to those who hold that view; this meaning should not be confused with the most common modern meaning, namely the fallacy of criticizing a controversial view by questioning the motives, character, or circumstances of those who hold it, instead of criticizing the reasons they offer.

annual motion. In the geostatic worldview, this was the orbital revolution of the sun around the central motionless earth, in an eastward direction relative to the fixed stars and taking one year to complete; in the Copernican system, this is simply the earth's orbital revolution around the sun, also in an eastward direction and lasting one year.

Aristarchus of Samos (c. 310–250 B.C.). Ancient Greek astronomer who elaborated the theory that the earth moves around the sun.

Attavanti, Giannozzo (c. 1582–1657). Minor cleric, not yet ordained priest, named in Caccini's deposition; interrogated by the Inquisition on 14 November 1615.

Barberini, Antonio (1569–1646). Brother of Maffeo Barberini, appointed cardinal with the title of Sant'Onofrio when his brother became Pope Urban VIII, one of the inquisitors conducting the trial in 1633, and secretary of the Inquisition at that time.

Barberini, Francesco (1597–1679). Nephew of Maffeo Barberini (Pope Urban VIII), appointed cardinal by the latter in 1623, and Vatican secretary of state during most of his papacy; also a patron of Galileo and of culture in general; and one of the inquisitors conducting the trial in 1633, but one of three who did not sign the final sentence.

Barberini, Maffeo (1568–1644). Member of an influential Florentine family; highly educated in such fields as philosophy, literature, and jurisprudence; held numerous diplomatic and ecclesiastic positions; cardinal beginning in 1606; elected Pope Urban VIII in 1623; at first a great admirer of Galileo, but their relationship soured after the publication of the *Dialogue* in 1632, which led to the trial and condemnation of the following year.

Baronio, Cesare (1538–1607). Cardinal beginning in 1596, reported by Galileo (in the *Letter to the Grand Duchess Christina*) as the author of the aphorism that "the intention of the Holy Spirit is to teach us how one goes to heaven and not how heaven goes."

Bellarmine, Robert (1542–1621). Jesuit theologian, perhaps the most influential Catholic churchman of his time, and now a saint; besides being a cardinal, he also served as a professor at the Roman College (the Jesuit university in Rome), an archbishop, the pope's theologian, a consultant to the Inquisition, and a member of both Congregations of the Inquisition and the Index.

Borgia, Gaspare (1589–1645). Spanish ambassador to Rome, cardinal beginning in 1611, and one of the three inquisitors conducting the trial in 1633 who did not sign the sentence.

Brahe, Tycho. See *Tycho Brahe.*

Buonamici, Giovanfrancesco (1592–1669). Tuscan diplomat and government official, who traveled widely in Germany, Austria, and Spain; also a distant relative of Galileo, being brother-in-law of Galileo's son, Vincenzio.

Caccini, Tommaso (1574–1648). Dominican friar from Florence, who held various administrative positions in his order and earned various academic degrees and positions in theology; accused Galileo of heresy in a sermon in 1614, and testified against him with the Inquisition in 1615.

Castelli, Benedetto (1578–1643). Benedictine monk, student of Galileo at the University of Padua, his successor at the University of Pisa, and friend and collaborator.

Cesi, Federico (1585–1630). Wealthy and influential Italian aristocrat, patron of the arts and sciences, and himself interested in writing about scientific subjects and doing scientific research; most famous as the founder and head of the Lincean Academy, the first international scientific society in modern science.

Christina of Lorraine (d. 1637). Wife of Ferdinando I de' Medici beginning in 1589, mother of Cosimo II de' Medici, grand duchess dowager after the death of Ferdinando in 1609, and a regent of the Grand Duchy when Cosimo died in 1621 while his successor Ferdinando II was still a minor.

Ciampoli, Giovanni (1589 or 1590–1643). Florentine intellectual, friend of Galileo, clergyman from November 1614, later a member of the Lincean Academy; a confidant of Cardinal Maffeo Barberini and his correspondence secretary when he became pope.

Cioli, Andrea (1573–1641). Tuscan secretary of state beginning in 1627.

Clavius, Christoph (1537–1612). German Jesuit, professor at the Jesuit Roman College in Rome, and one of the leading mathematicians and astronomers of his time; was on friendly terms with Galileo.

Cosimo II de' Medici (1590–1621). Ruler of the Grand Duchy of Tuscany from 1609 to 1621.

Diodati, Elia (1576–1661). French Protestant born in Geneva; lawyer for the Paris Parliament; old friend and strong supporter of Galileo; responsible for the publication in Strasbourg of Latin translations of the *Dialogue* (1635) and the *Letter to Christina* (1636).

diurnal motion. At the level of observation, diurnal motion is the apparent motion of all heavenly bodies around the earth, occurring every day in a westward direction; in the geostatic worldview, such apparent motion corresponds to reality; in the Copernican system, the diurnal motion is simply the earth's daily rotation around its own axis, in an *eastward* direction.

eccentric. An eccentric was a circular orbit of one heavenly body around another, but such that the second body is not located at the geometrical center of the orbit but off that center; this device enables the distance between the two bodies to vary.

ecliptic. A term used to denote the annual orbit of the sun around the earth (in the geostatic system), or of the earth around the sun (in the Copernican system); the term also denotes the plane on which the annual orbit lies, and the circle resulting from projecting the annual orbit onto the celestial sphere.

Ecphantus. Ancient Greek who lived in Syracuse at the beginning of the fifth century B.C. and advocated the geokinetic view.

epicycle. A circle whose center lies on and moves along the circumference of a larger circle, called deferent; the postulation of epicycles enabled astronomers to analyze the motion of heavenly bodies as a combination of circular motions, so that there would be variations in the distance from the heavenly body to the center of the deferent, as well as in the body's direction of motion as seen from that center.

Firenzuola, Vincenzo da. See *Maculano, Vincenzo*.

fixed star. A heavenly body that is visible normally only at night and appears to revolve daily around the earth without changing its position relative to other stars; thus, all fixed stars appear to move in unison as if they were fixed on a celestial sphere, whose daily rotation carries them all along; a fixed star corresponds to what is nowadays called simply *star*, but in Galileo's time *star* meant simply *heavenly body* and stars were divided into fixed and wandering.

Foscarini, Paolo Antonio (1580–1616). Head of the order of Carmelites in the province of Calabria and professor of theology at the University of Messina; published in early 1615 a book that showed the compatibility between the Bible and the earth's motion; this book was condemned and totally banned by the Index's Decree of 1616.

geokinetic. Pertaining to the earth's motion or claiming that the earth moves; the geokinetic worldview claims that the earth rotates daily on its axis from west to east and revolves yearly around the sun in the same direction; this term is contrasted with the term *geostatic* and may be taken to correspond to *Copernican*.

Gondi, Giovanni Battista (1589–1664). Tuscan secretary of state beginning in 1636.

Guicciardini, Piero (1560–1626). Tuscan ambassador to the Holy See from 1611 to 1621.

Holy Office. See *Inquisition.*

Index. Short for the Congregation of the Index, the department of the Catholic Church in charge of book censorship; created in 1571 by Pope Pius V, it was meant to formalize the periodic publication of the *Index of Prohibited Books,* whose first edition had already appeared in 1564 as a result of the Council of Trent; nowadays, this department no longer exists.

Inquisition. The common name for the Congregation of the Holy Office, the department of the Catholic Church whose purpose was to defend and uphold faith and morals; instituted in 1542 by Pope Paul III, it was meant to take over the suppression of heresies and heretics begun by the medieval Inquisition; by the time of Galileo, the notion of heresy had been given a legal definition and inquisitorial procedures had been codified; nowadays, this department is called Congregation for the Doctrine of the Faith.

Jupiter. A planet whose orbit is bigger than the annual orbit and whose period of revolution is about twelve years.

Kepler, Johannes (1571–1630). Mathematician to the Holy Roman emperor, and a leading proponent of Copernicanism, which he elaborated in new and important ways; most famous for the three laws of planetary motion named after him, the first of which states that the planets move around the sun in elliptical orbits, with the sun located at one of the foci of these ellipses; one of the first and strongest supporters of Galileo's telescopic discoveries, though Galileo never did reciprocate in kind and did not even pay attention to his laws of planetary motion.

Lincean Academy. Also called Academy of the Linceans, which means literally "academy of those who have lynx eyes"; the first modern international scientific academy, having been founded in 1603 by Federico Cesi, although it fell apart soon after his death. Galileo was made a member in 1611 and received support from the Academy for the publication of many of his works.

Lorini, Niccolò (b. 1544). Born in Florence, died at an uncertain date after 1617; Dominican friar who held various administrative posts in various convents; highly regarded as a preacher; became professor of Church history at the University of Florence.

Maculano, Vincenzo (1578–1667). Also known as Vincenzo da Firenzuola, from his native town; became a Dominican friar, general of his order, Master of the Sacred Palace, and cardinal; well known as a skillful military construction engineer; and best known as the commissary general of the Inquisition at the time of the 1633 proceedings.

Medicean planets. A term used by Galileo to refer to Jupiter's satellites, which he discovered; he named the new bodies in honor of Cosimo II de' Medici, who ruled Florence and the Grand Duchy of Tuscany.

Niccolini, Francesco (1584–1650). Tuscan ambassador to the Holy See from 1621 to 1643.

orb. A term that is partly synonymous with the term *orbit,* namely the path followed by one heavenly body around another; the term also refers to the region of the heavens where a given orbital path is located.

orbit. The path followed by a heavenly body as it moves among the other bodies, usually around some particular body or point that is regarded as the center or focus of the orbit.

Peiresc, Nicolas Claude Fabri de (1580–1637). French lawyer, politician, diplomat, and amateur natural philosopher; became acquainted with Galileo personally in Padua, when the latter taught at the university there; was on very good terms with the Barberini family, and hosted at his own house Cardinal Francesco Barberini, when the latter was returning from Paris to Rome on a special diplomatic mission in 1625.

Picchena, Curzio (1553–1626). Tuscan secretary of state beginning in 1613.

planet. A term originating from Greek, meaning a "wandering" star, namely a heavenly body that appears to move both around the earth and in relation to other heavenly bodies; thus, it appears to perform simultaneously two motions around the earth, the diurnal motion from east to west every day, and another revolution from west to east in a definite period of time varying from one planet to another. In the geostatic worldview, there were seven planets, their arrangement in the order of increasing orbit and period being: moon, Mercury, Venus, sun, Mars, Jupiter, and Saturn. In the Copernican system, the planets were: Mercury, Venus, earth, Mars, Jupiter, and Saturn; whereas the sun was the center of planetary orbits, and the moon was merely the earth's satellite.

Prime Mobile. A term meant to convey the idea of the "first body in motion"; in Aristotelian natural philosophy, the Prime Mobile was a sphere lying outside the celestial sphere and acted upon by the First Unmoved Mover; by rotating daily from east to west, the Prime Mobile carried along all the other heavenly bodies (except the earth), giving them their diurnal motion.

Riccardi, Niccolò (1585–1639). Dominican friar, and beginning in 1629 Master of the Sacred Palace; this was the office in charge of book censorship in Rome.

Sagredo, Giovanfrancesco (1571–1620). Venetian aristocrat and diplomat who became Galileo's best friend when Galileo taught at the University of Padua; immortalized as one of the three speakers in the *Dialogue* and the *Two New Sciences.*

Salviati, Filippo (1582–1614). Wealthy Florentine nobleman whose interest in science and philosophy earned him membership in the Lincean Academy in 1612; one of Galileo's closest friends in Florence; immortalized as one of the three characters in the *Dialogue* and the *Two New Sciences.*

Sarpi, Paolo (1552–1623). Venetian, member of the Servite order, lawyer, theologian, historian, and natural philosopher; became the official theologian of the Republic of Venice; leader in the struggles between the Venetian Republic and the papacy, and more generally in the establishment of the principle of separation of Church and State; author of a famous history of the Council of Trent, published under a pseudonym in London in 1619, and critical of papal absolutism and centralization. Galileo and Sarpi became friends during the eighteen years that Galileo taught at the University of Padua, which is near Venice and was a public institution financially supported by the Venetian Republic.

save the appearances (or the phenomena). To explain observed natural phenomena by means of assumptions that are taken not necessarily to describe real physical processes, but rather to be primarily convenient instruments for making mathematical calculations and observational predictions.

Scheiner, Christoph (1573–1650). German Jesuit astronomer who discovered sunspots at about the same time as Galileo, but interpreted them in an Aristotelian, Ptolemaic framework; was involved in a bitter dispute with Galileo over priority of discovery and over their interpretation.

Sfondrati, Paolo (1561–1618). Cardinal with the title of Santa Cecilia; head of the Congregation of the Index and member of the Congregation of the Holy Office at the time of the earlier proceedings against Galileo; at various times, Bishop of Cremona and Bishop of Albano.

Simplicio. Name of one of the three characters in the *Dialogue* and the *Two New Sciences;* Italian word denoting a simpleton, as well as the philosopher Simplicius, who lived in the sixth century A.D. and is one of the greatest commentators of Aristotle.

Tycho Brahe (1546–1601). Danish astronomer, best known as an excellent observer and collector of data; promoter of the so-called Tychonic system, according to which the earth is motionless at the center of the universe, the planets revolve around the sun, but the sun (together with all the planets) moves around the earth, daily in a westward direction and annually in an eastward direction. Kepler worked with him and inherited his data.

Urban VIII. See *Barberini, Maffeo.*

Venus. A planet that revolves in its orbit in such a way that it always appears close to the sun. With the telescope, Galileo discovered the phases of Venus, which are changes in its apparent shape similar to those which the moon exhibits each month; this proved conclusively that Venus revolves around the sun; but this confirmed the system of Tycho Brahe as well as that of Copernicus, and so the choice between these two systems required other evidence for a conclusive demonstration.

wandering star. Heavenly body that appears not only to revolve daily around the earth, but also to change its position relative to other heavenly bodies; that is, it wanders around in the heavens according to a period that characterizes each wandering star; hence, it is equivalent to *planet,* a Greek word whose literal meaning is *wandering star;* contrasted to *fixed star.*

Ximenes, Emanuele (b. 1542). A Jesuit named in Caccini's deposition; consultant to the Inquisition in Florence at the time of the earlier proceedings; died at an uncertain date soon thereafter.

Ximenes, Ferdinando (c. 1580–1630). Dominican named in Caccini's deposition, who was interrogated by the Inquisition on 13 November 1615.

Ximenes, Sebastiano. Founder in 1583 of the Order of the Knights of Santo Stefano; named in Caccini's deposition.

zodiac. Narrow belt on the celestial sphere along which the planets, sun, and moon appear to move; subdivided into twelve equal parts of thirty degrees each, each part being the location of a group of stars arranged into a distinct pattern. These twelve patterns are the constellations of the zodiac: Aries, Taurus, Gemini, Cancer, Leo, Virgo, Libra, Scorpio, Sagittarius, Capricornus, Aquarius, and Pisces; this order corresponds to an eastward direction (from the viewpoint of terrestrial observation).

Selected Bibliography

Aquinas, Thomas. 1952. *Summa theologica*. 2 vols. Chicago: Encyclopedia Britannica.

Beltrán Marí, Antonio. 2006. *Talento y poder.* Pamplona: Laetoli.

Beretta, Francesco. 1998. *Galilée devant le Tribunal de l'Inquisition*. Doctoral Dissertation, Faculty of Theology, University of Fribourg, Switzerland.

———. 1999. "Le Procès de Galilée et les Archives du Saint-Office." *Revue des Sciences Philosophiques et Théologiques* 83: 441–90.

———. 2005a. "The Documents of Galileo's Trial." In McMullin 2005, 191–212.

———. 2005b. "Galileo, Urban VIII, and the Prosecution of Natural Philosophers." In McMullin 2005, 234–61.

———, ed. 2005c. *Galilée en procès, Galilée réhabilité?* Saint-Maurice: Éditions Saint-Augustin.

Berti, Domenico. 1876. *Il processo originale di Galileo Galilei pubblicato per la prima volta*. Rome.

Biagioli, Mario. 1993. *Galileo Courtier*. Chicago: University of Chicago Press.

———. 2006. *Galileo's Instruments of Credit*. Chicago: University of Chicago Press.

Blackwell, Richard J. 1991. *Galileo, Bellarmine, and the Bible*. Notre Dame: University of Notre Dame Press.

———. 2006. *Behind the Scenes at Galileo's Trial*. Notre Dame: University of Notre Dame Press.

Bucciantini, Massimo. 1995. *Contro Galileo*. Florence: Olschki.

Bucciantini, Massimo, and Michele Camerota, trans. and eds. 2009. *Scienza e religione*. Rome: Donzelli.

Camerota, Michele. 2004. *Galileo Galilei e la cultura scientifica nell'età della Controriforma*. Rome: Salerno Editrice.

Copernicus, Nicolaus. 1992. *On the Revolutions*. Translated and edited by E. Rosen. Baltimore: Johns Hopkins University Press.

Damanti, Alfredo. 2010. *Libertas philosophandi*. Rome: Edizioni di Storia e Letteratura.

Dershowitz, Alan. 1991. "Introduction." In Finocchiaro 1991.

DiCanzio, Albert. 1996. *Galileo: His Science and His Significance for the Future of Man*. Portsmouth: Adasi.

Eymericus, Nicolaus. 1578/1973. *Le manuel des inquisiteurs*. Commentary by Francisco Peña. Translated and edited by Louis Sala-Molins. Paris: Mouton.

Fantoli, Annibale. 2003. *Galileo*. 3rd ed. Translated by G.V. Coyne. Vatican City: Vatican Observatory Publications.

———. 2012. *The Case of Galileo*. Translated by G.V. Coyne. Notre Dame: University of Notre Dame Press.

Favaro, Antonio, ed. 1890–1909. *Opere di Galileo Galilei*. [Same as Galilei 1890–1909.]

Feldhay, Rivka. 1995. *Galileo and the Church*. Cambridge: Cambridge University Press.

———. 2000. "Recent Narratives on Galileo and the Church: or the Three Dogmas of the Counter-Reformation." *Science in Context* 13: 489–507.

Finocchiaro, Maurice A. 1980. *Galileo and the Art of Reasoning: Rhetorical Foundations of Logic and Scientific Method*. Dordrecht: Reidel.

———, trans. and ed. 1989. *The Galileo Affair: A Documentary History*. Berkeley: University of California Press.

———, trans. and ed. 1991. *The Galileo Affair: A Documentary History*. Special ed., in the Notable Trials Library. New York: Gryphon Editions.

———. 2002. "Philosophy versus Religion and Science versus Religion: The Trials of Bruno and Galileo." In *Giordano Bruno,* edited by Hilary Gatti, 51–96. Aldershot: Ashgate.

———. 2005. *Retrying Galileo, 1633–1992*. Berkeley: University of California Press.

———. 2009. "Myth 8: That Galileo Was Imprisoned and Tortured for Advocating Copernicanism." In *Galileo Goes to Jail and Other Myths about Science and Religion,* edited by Ronald L. Numbers, 68–78, 249–52. Cambridge, MA: Harvard University Press.

———. 2010. *Defending Copernicus and Galileo: Critical Reasoning in the Two Affairs*. Dordrecht: Springer.

———. 2011. "Fair-mindedness vs. Sophistry in the Galileo Affair." In *Controversies within the Scientific Revolution,* edited by Marcelo Dascal and V. Boantza, 53–73. Amsterdam: John Benjamins.

———. 2013. "Galileo under Fire and under Patronage." In *Ideas under Fire,* edited by Jonathan Lavery, L. Groarke, and W. Sweet, 123–43. Lanham, MD: Rowman & Littlefield.

———. 2014. *Routledge Guidebook to Galileo's* Dialogue. London: Routledge.

Galilei, Galileo. 1890–1909. *Opere*. 20 vols. National Edition by A. Favaro et al. Florence: Barbèra.

———. 1997. *Galileo on the World Systems: A New Abridged Translation and Guide*. Translated and edited by M. A. Finocchiaro. Berkeley: University of California Press.

———. 2008. *The Essential Galileo*. Translated and edited by M. A. Finocchiaro. Indianapolis: Hackett Publishing Company.

Gingerich, Owen. 1982. "The Galileo Affair." *Scientific American,* August, pp. 132–43.

Heilbron, John L. 2010. *Galileo.* Oxford: Oxford University Press.

———. 2012. "The *Bizzarrie* of the *Dialogo.*" *Galilaeana* 9: 29–64.

Jerome, Saint. 1893. *Letters and Select Works.* Translated by W.H. Fremantle. New York.

Koestler, Arthur. 1959. *The Sleepwalkers.* New York: Macmillan.

———. 1964. "The Greatest Scandal in Christendom." *The Observer* (London), February 2, pp. 21, 29.

Masini, Eliseo. 1621. *Sacro arsenale, overo prattica dell'officio della Santa Inquisitione.* Genoa.

Mayaud, Pierre-Noël. 1997. *La condamnation des livres coperniciens.* Rome: Editrice Pontificia Università Gregoriana.

———, ed. 2005. *Le conflit entre l'astronomie nouvelle et l'Écriture Sainte aux XVIᵉ et XVIIᵉ siècles.* 6 vols. Paris: Honoré Champion.

Mayer, Thomas F., trans. and ed. 2012. *The Trial of Galileo 1612–1633.* Toronto: University of Toronto Press.

———. 2013. *The Roman Inquisition.* Philadelphia: University of Pennsylvania Press.

McMullin, Ernan, ed. 2005. *The Church and Galileo.* Notre Dame: University of Notre Dame Press.

Miller, David M. 2008. "The Thirty Years War and the Galileo Affair." *History of Science* 46: 49–74.

Mourant, John A., ed. 1964. *Introduction to the Philosophy of Saint Augustine.* University Park: Pennsylvania State University Press.

Pagano, Sergio, ed. 2009. *I documenti vaticani del processo di Galileo Galilei (1611–1741).* Vatican City: Archivio Segreto Vaticano.

Pastor, Ludwig von. 1898–1953. *History of Popes from the Close of the Middle Ages.* 40 vols. Translated by E.F. Peeler. Saint Louis: Herder.

Pesce, Mauro. 1992. "Le redazioni originali della Lettera 'copernicana' di G. Galilei a B. Castelli." *Filologia e critica* 17: 394–417.

Ranke, Leopold von. 1841. *The Ecclesiastical and Political History of the Popes of Rome.* 2 vols. Translated by S. Austin. Philadelphia.

Redondi, Pietro. 1987. *Galileo Heretic.* Translated by R. Rosenthal. Princeton: Princeton University Press.

Reeves, Eileen, and Albert van Helden, trans. and eds. 2010. *On Sunspots.* Chicago: University of Chicago Press.

Rosen, Edward. 1958. "Galileo's Misstatements about Copernicus." *Isis* 49: 319–30.

———. 1975. "Was Copernicus's *Revolutions* Approved by the Pope?" *Journal of the History of Ideas* 36: 531–42.

Russo, François. 1968. "Lettre de Galilée à Christine de Lorraine." In *Galilée: Aspects de sa vie et de son oeuvre,* 324–59. Paris: Presses Universitaires de France.

Scaglia, Desiderio. 1616?/1986. *Prattica per proceder nelle cause del Santo Uffitio.* In Alfonso Mirto, "Un inedito del Seicento sull' Inquisizione," *Nouvelles de la République des Lettres,* 1986, no. 1, pp. 99–138.

Segre, Michael. 1991. "Science at the Tuscan Court, 1642–1667." In *Physics, Cosmology and Astronomy, 1300–1700,* edited by S. Unguru, 295–308. Dordrecht: Kluwer.

Sobel, Dava. 1999. *Galileo's Daughter.* New York: Walker & Company.

Speller, Jules. 2008. *Galileo's Inquisition Trial Revisited.* Frankfurt: Peter Lang.

Tertullian, Quintus S. F. 1972. *Adversus Marcionem.* Translated and edited by E. Evans. Oxford: Clarendon.

Westfall, Richard S. 1984. "Galileo and the Accademia dei Lincei." In *Novità celesti e crisi del sapere,* edited by Paolo Galluzzi, 189–200. Florence: Giunti Barbèra.

———. 1985. "Science and Patronage." *Isis* 76: 11–30.

———. 1989. *Essays on the Trial of Galileo.* Notre Dame: University of Notre Dame Press.

Westman, Robert S. 2011. *The Copernican Question.* Berkeley: University of California Press.

CHAPTER 1

Theological Issues:
Copernicanism vs. Scripture

§1. Galileo's Letter to Castelli (21 December 1613)[1]

[281] Yesterday Mr. Niccolò Arrighetti came to visit me and told me about you. Thus I took infinite pleasure in hearing about what I did not doubt at all, namely about the great satisfaction you have been giving to the whole University, to its administrators as well as to the professors themselves and to the students from all countries. This approval has not increased the number of your rivals, as it usually happens in similar cases, but rather they have been reduced to very few; and these few too will have to acquiesce unless they want this competition (which is sometimes called a virtue) to degenerate and to change into a blameworthy and harmful feeling, harmful ultimately more to those who practice it than to anyone else. However, the seal of my pleasure was to hear him relate the arguments which, through the great kindness of their Most Serene Highnesses, you had the occasion of advancing at their table and then of continuing in the chambers of the Most Serene Ladyship, in the presence also of the Grand Duke and the Most Serene Archduchess, the Most Illustrious and Excellent Don Antonio and Don Paolo Giordano, and some of the very excellent philosophers there. What greater fortune can you wish than to see their Highnesses themselves enjoying discussing with you, putting forth doubts, listening to your solutions, and finally remaining satisfied with your answers?

[282] After Mr. Arrighetti related the details you had mentioned, they gave me the occasion to go back to examine some general questions about the use of the Holy Scripture in disputes involving physical conclusions and some particular other ones about Joshua's passage,[2] which was presented in opposition to the earth's motion and sun's stability by the Grand Duchess Dowager with some support by the Most Serene Archduchess.

In regard to the first general point of the Most Serene Ladyship, it seems to me very prudent of her to propose and of you to concede and to agree that the Holy Scripture can never lie or err, and that its declarations are absolutely

---

1. Reprinted from Finocchiaro 1989, 49–54; cf. Galilei 1890–1909, 5: 281–88.
2. Joshua 10:12–13; I quote this passage in the Introduction (§0.3), above.

and inviolably true. I should have added only that, though Scripture cannot err, nevertheless some of its interpreters and expositors can sometimes err in various ways. One of these would be very serious and very frequent, namely to want to limit oneself always to the literal meaning of the words; for there would thus emerge not only various contradictions but also serious heresies and blasphemies, and it would be necessary to attribute to God feet, hands, and eyes, as well as bodily and human feelings like anger, regret, hate, and sometimes even forgetfulness of things past and ignorance of future ones. Thus in Scripture one finds many propositions which look different from the truth if one goes by the literal meaning of the words, but which are expressed in this manner to accommodate the incapacity of common people; likewise, for the few who deserve to be separated from the masses, it is necessary that wise interpreters produce their true meaning and indicate the particular reasons why they have been expressed by means of such words.

Thus, given that in many places Scripture is not only capable but necessarily in need of interpretations different from the apparent meaning of the words, it seems to me that in disputes about natural phenomena it should be reserved to the last place. For the Holy Scripture and nature both equally derive from the divine Word, the former as the dictation of the Holy Spirit, the latter as the most obedient executrix of God's commands; moreover, in order to adapt itself to the understanding of all people, it was appropriate for Scripture to say many things [283] which are different from absolute truth, in appearance and in regard to the meaning of the words; on the other hand, nature is inexorable and immutable, and she does not care at all whether or not her recondite reasons and modes of operations are revealed to human understanding, and so she never transgresses the terms of the laws imposed on her; therefore, whatever sensory experience places before our eyes or necessary demonstrations prove to us concerning natural effects should not in any way be called into question on account of scriptural passages whose words appear to have a different meaning, since not every statement of Scripture is bound to obligations as severely as each effect of nature. Indeed, because of the aim of adapting itself to the capacity of unrefined and undisciplined peoples, Scripture has not abstained from somewhat concealing its most basic dogmas, thus attributing to God himself properties contrary to and very far from his essence; so who will categorically maintain that, in speaking even incidentally of the earth or the sun or other creatures, it abandoned this aim and chose to restrict itself rigorously within the limited and narrow meanings of the words? This would have been especially problematic when saying about these creatures things which are very far from the primary function of the Holy Writ, indeed things which, if said and put forth in their naked and unadorned truth, would more likely harm its primary intention and make people more resistant to persuasion about the articles pertaining to salvation.

Given this, and moreover it being obvious that two truths can never contradict each other, the task of wise interpreters is to strive to find the true
meanings of scriptural passages agreeing with those physical conclusions of
which we are already certain and sure from clear sensory experience or from
necessary demonstrations. Furthermore, as I already said, though Scripture
was inspired by the Holy Spirit, because of the mentioned reasons many passages admit of interpretations far removed from the literal meaning, and also
we cannot assert with certainty that all interpreters speak by divine inspiration; hence, I should believe that it would be prudent not to allow anyone
to oblige [284] scriptural passages to have to maintain the truth of any physical conclusions whose contrary could ever be shown to us by the senses and
demonstrative and necessary reasons. Who wants to fix a limit for the human
mind? Who wants to assert that everything which is knowable in the world
is already known? Because of this, it would be most advisable not to add anything beyond necessity to the articles concerning salvation and the definition
of the Faith, which are firm enough that there is no danger of any valid and
effective doctrine ever rising against them. If this is so, what greater disorder
would result from adding them upon request by persons of whom we do not
know whether they speak with celestial inspiration, and of whom also we see
clearly that they are completely lacking in the intelligence needed to understand, let alone to criticize, the demonstrations by means of which the most
exact sciences proceed in the confirmation of some of their conclusions?

I should believe that the authority of the Holy Writ has merely the aim
of persuading men of those articles and propositions which are necessary for
their salvation and surpass all human reason, and so could not become credible through some other science or any other means except the mouth of the
Holy Spirit itself. However, I do not think it necessary to believe that the same
God who has furnished us with senses, language, and intellect would want to
bypass their use and give us by other means the information we can obtain
with them. This applies especially to those sciences about which one can read
only very small phrases and scattered conclusions in Scripture, as is particularly
the case for astronomy, of which it contains such a small portion that one does
not even find in it the names of all the planets; but if the first sacred writers
had been thinking of persuading the people about the arrangement and the
movements of the heavenly bodies, they would not have treated of them so
sparsely, which is to say almost [285] nothing in comparison to the infinity of
very lofty and admirable conclusions contained in such a science.

So you see, if I am not mistaken, how disorderly is the procedure of those
who in disputes about natural phenomena that do not directly involve the
Faith give first place to scriptural passages, which they quite often misunder-
stand anyway. However, if these people really believe to have grasped the
true meaning of a particular scriptural passage, and if they consequently feel

sure of possessing the absolute truth on the question they intend to dispute about, then let them sincerely tell me whether they think that in a natural dispute someone who happens to maintain the truth has a great advantage over another who happens to maintain the false. I know they will answer Yes, and that the one who supports the true side will be able to provide a thousand experiments and a thousand necessary demonstrations for his side, whereas the other person can have nothing but sophisms, paralogisms, and fallacies. But if they know they have such an advantage over their opponents as long as the discussion is limited to physical questions and only philosophical weapons are used, why is it that when they come to the meeting they immediately introduce an irresistible and terrible weapon, the mere sight of which terrifies even the most skillful and expert champion? If I must tell the truth, I believe it is they who are the most terrified, and that they are trying to find a way of not letting the opponent approach because they feel unable to resist his assaults. However, consider that, as I just said, whoever has truth on his side has a great, indeed the greatest, advantage over the opponent, and that it is impossible for two truths to contradict each other; it follows therefore that we must not fear any assaults launched against us by anyone, as long as we are allowed to speak and to be heard by competent persons who are not excessively upset by their own emotions and interests.

To confirm this, I now come to examining the specific passage of Joshua, concerning which you put forth three theses for their Most Serene Highnesses. I take the third one, which you advanced as mine (as indeed it is), but I add some other consideration which I do not believe I have ever told you.

Let us then assume and concede to the opponent that the words [286] of the sacred text should be taken precisely in their literal meaning, namely that in answer to Joshua's prayers God made the sun stop and lengthened the day, so that as a result he achieved victory; but I request that the same rule should apply to both, so that the opponent should not pretend to tie me and to leave himself free to change or modify the meanings of the words. Given this, I say that this passage shows clearly the falsity and impossibility of the Aristotelian and Ptolemaic world system, and on the other hand agrees very well with the Copernican one.

I first ask the opponent whether he knows with how many motions the sun moves. If he knows, he must answer that it moves with two motions, namely with the annual motion from west to east and with the diurnal motion in the opposite direction from east to west.

Then, secondly, I ask him whether these two motions, so different and almost contrary to each other, belong to the sun and are its own to an equal extent. The answer must be No, but that only one is specifically its own, namely the annual motion, whereas the other is not but belongs to the highest heaven, I mean the Prime Mobile; the latter carries along with it the sun as well as the other planets and the stellar sphere, forcing them to make a revolution around the earth in twenty-four hours, with a motion, as I said, almost contrary to their own natural motion.

Coming to the third question, I ask him with which of these two motions the sun produces night and day, that is, whether with its own motion or else with that of the Prime Mobile. The answer must be that night and day are effects of the motion of the Prime Mobile, and that what depends on the sun's own motion is not night and day but the various seasons and the year itself.

Now, if the day derives not from the sun's motion but from that of the Prime Mobile, who does not see that to lengthen the day one must stop the Prime Mobile and not the sun? Indeed, is there anyone who understands these first elements of astronomy and does not know that, if God had stopped the sun's motion, He would have cut and shortened the day instead of lengthening it? For, the sun's motion being [287] contrary to the diurnal turning, the more the sun moves toward the east the more its progression toward the west is slowed down, whereas by its motion being diminished or annihilated the sun would set that much sooner; this phenomenon is observed in the moon, whose diurnal revolutions are slower than those of the sun inasmuch as its own motion is faster than that of the sun. It follows that it is absolutely impossible to stop the sun and lengthen the day in the system of Ptolemy and Aristotle, and therefore either the motions must not be arranged as Ptolemy says or we must modify the meaning of the words of Scripture; we would have to claim that, when it says that God stopped the sun, it meant to say that He stopped the Prime Mobile, and that it said the contrary of what it would have said if speaking to educated men in order to adapt itself to the capacity of those who are barely able to understand the rising and setting of the sun.

Add to this that it is not believable that God would stop only the sun, letting the other spheres proceed; for He would have unnecessarily altered and upset all the order, appearances, and arrangements of the other stars in relation to the sun, and would have greatly disturbed the whole system of nature. On the other hand, it is believable that He would stop the whole system of celestial spheres, which could then together return to their operations without any confusion or change after the period of intervening rest.

However, we have already agreed not to change the meaning of the words in the text; therefore it is necessary to resort to another arrangement of the parts of the world, and to see whether the literal meaning of the words flows directly and without obstacle from its point of view. This is in fact what we see happening.

For I have discovered and conclusively demonstrated that the [288] solar globe turns on itself,[3] completing an entire rotation in about one lunar month,

---

3. Galilei 1890–1909, 5: 133–35; 2008, 97–99.

in exactly the same direction as all the other heavenly revolutions; moreover, it is very probable and reasonable that, as the chief instrument and minister of nature and almost the heart of the world, the sun gives not only light (as it obviously does) but also motion to all the planets that revolve around it; hence, if in conformity with Copernicus's position the diurnal motion is attributed to the earth, anyone can see that it sufficed stopping the sun to stop the whole system, and thus to lengthen the period of the diurnal illumination without altering in any way the rest of the mutual relationships of the planets; and that is exactly how the words of the sacred text sound. Here then is the manner in which by stopping the sun one can lengthen the day on the earth, without introducing any confusion among the parts of the world and without altering the words of Scripture.

I have written much more than is appropriate in view of my slight illness. So I end by reminding you that I am at your service, and I kiss your hands and pray the Lord to give you happy holidays and all you desire.

§2. Galileo's *Letter to the Grand Duchess Christina* (1615)[4]

[309] [§2.1] As Your Most Serene Highness knows very well, a few years ago I discovered in the heavens many particulars which had been invisible until our time. Because of their novelty, and because of some consequences deriving from them which contradict some physical propositions commonly accepted in philosophical schools, they roused against me no small number of such professors, as if I had placed these things in heaven with my hands in order to mess up nature and the sciences. These people seemed to forget that a multitude of truths contribute to inquiry and to the growth and strength of disciplines rather than to their diminution or destruction, and at the same time they showed greater affection for their own opinions than for the true ones; thus they proceeded to deny and to try to nullify those novelties, about which the senses themselves could have rendered them certain, if they had wanted to look at those novelties carefully. To this end they produced various matters, and they published some writings full of useless discussions and sprinkled with quotations from the Holy Scripture, taken from passages which they do not properly understand and which they inappropriately adduce. This was a very serious error, and they might not have fallen into it had they paid attention to Saint Augustine's very useful advice [310] concerning how to proceed with care in reaching definite decisions about things which are obscure and difficult to understand by means of reason alone. For, speaking also about a particular physical conclusion pertaining to heavenly bodies, he writes this

---

4. Reprinted from Finocchiaro 1989, 87–118; cf. Galilei 1890–1909, 5: 309–48.

(*On the Literal Interpretation of Genesis*, book 2, at the end): "Now then, always practicing a pious and serious moderation, we ought not to believe anything lightly about an obscure subject, lest we reject (out of love for our error) something which later may be truly shown not to be in any way contrary to the holy books of either the Old or New Testament."[5]

Then it developed that the passage of time disclosed to everyone the truths I had first pointed out, and, along with the truth of the matter, the difference in attitude between those who sincerely and without envy did not accept these discoveries as true and those who added emotional agitation to disbelief. Thus, just as those who were most competent in astronomical and in physical science were convinced by my first announcement, so gradually there has been a calming down of all the others whose denials and doubts were not sustained by anything other than the unexpected novelty and the lack of opportunity to see them and to experience them with the senses. However, there are those who are rendered ill–disposed, not so much toward the things as much as toward the author, by the love of their first error and by some interest which they imagine having but which escapes me. Unable to deny them any longer, these people became silent about them; but, embittered more than before by what has mellowed and quieted the others, they divert their thinking to other fictions and try to harm me in other ways. These would not really worry me any more than I was disturbed by the other oppositions, which I always laughed off, certain of the result that the business would have; I should not worry if I did not see that the new calumnies and persecutions are not limited to matters of greater or less theoretical understanding, which are relatively unimportant, but that they go further and try to damage me with stains which I do abhor and must abhor more than death. Nor can I be satisfied that these charges be known as false only by those who know me and them; their falsity must be known to every other person.

These people are aware that in my [311] astronomical and philosophical studies, on the question of the constitution of the world's parts, I hold that the sun is located at the center of the revolutions of the heavenly orbs and does not change place, and that the earth rotates on itself and moves around it. Moreover, they hear how I confirm this view not only by refuting Ptolemy's and Aristotle's arguments, but also by producing many for the other side, especially some pertaining to physical effects whose causes perhaps cannot be determined in any other way, and other astronomical ones dependent on many features of the new celestial discoveries; these discoveries clearly confute the Ptolemaic system, and they agree admirably with this other position and confirm it. Now, these people are perhaps confounded by the known truth of

---

5. Here and elsewhere, Galileo usually quotes such passages in Latin, and I usually translate his Latin quotations, unless I indicate otherwise in a note.

the other propositions different from the ordinary which I hold, and so they may lack confidence to defend themselves as long as they remain in the philosophical field. Therefore, since they persist in their original self-appointed task of beating down me and my findings by every imaginable means, they have decided to try to shield the fallacies of their arguments with the cloak of simulated religiousness and with the authority of the Holy Scriptures, unintelligently using the latter for the confutation of arguments they neither understand nor have heard.

At first, they tried on their own to spread among common people the idea that such propositions are against the Holy Scriptures, and consequently damnable and heretical. Then they realized how by and large human nature is more inclined to join those ventures which result in the oppression of other people (even if unjustly) than those which result in their just improvement, and so it was not difficult for them to find someone who with unusual confidence did preach even from the pulpit that it is damnable and heretical; and this was done with little compassion and with little consideration of the injury not only to this doctrine and its followers, but also to mathematics and all mathematicians. Thus, having acquired more confidence, and with the vain hope that that seed which first took root in their insincere mind would grow into a tree and rise toward the sky, they are spreading among the people the rumor that it will shortly be declared heretical by the supreme authority. They know that such a declaration not only would uproot these two conclusions, but also would render damnable all the other astronomical and physical observations and propositions [312] which correspond and are necessarily connected with them.

They alleviate their task as much as they can by making it look, at least among common people, as if this opinion were new and especially mine, pretending not to know that Nicolaus Copernicus was its author or rather its reformer and confirmer. Now, Copernicus was not only a Catholic, but also a clergyman[6] and a canon, and he was so highly regarded that he was called to Rome from the remotest parts of Germany[7] when under Leo X the Lateran Council was discussing the reform of the ecclesiastical calendar; at that time this reform remained unfinished only because there was still no exact knowledge of the precise length of the year and of the lunar month. Thus he was charged by the Bishop of Fossombrone,[8] who was then supervising this undertaking, to try by repeated studies and efforts to acquire more understanding and certainty about those celestial motions; and so he undertook this study, and, by truly

---

6. Here and in the rest of this paragraph, Galileo makes a number of misstatements about Copernicus; for example, although Copernicus was a canon and hence a type of cleric, he was not a clergyman in the sense of being a priest; cf. Rosen (1958; 1975).

7. Actually Poland.

8. Paul of Middelburg (1445–1533).

Herculean labor and by his admirable mind, he made so much progress in this science and acquired such an exact knowledge of the periods of celestial motions that he earned the title of supreme astronomer; then in accordance with his doctrine not only was the calendar regularized, but tables of all planetary motions were constructed. Having expounded this doctrine in six parts, he published it at the request of the Cardinal of Capua[9] and of the Bishop of Kulm;[10] and since he had undertaken this task and these labors on orders from the Supreme Pontiff, he dedicated his book *On Heavenly Revolutions* to the successor of the latter, Paul III. Once printed this book was accepted by the Holy Church, and it was read and studied all over the world, without anyone ever having had the least scruple about its doctrine. Finally, now that one is discovering how well founded upon clear observations and necessary demonstrations this doctrine is, some persons come along who, without having even seen the book, give its author the reward of so much work by trying to have him declared a heretic; this they do only in order to satisfy their special animosity, groundlessly conceived [313] against someone else who has no greater connection with Copernicus than the endorsement of his doctrine.

Now, in matters of religion and of reputation I have the greatest regard for how common people judge and view me; so, because of the false aspersions my enemies so unjustly try to cast upon me, I have thought it necessary to justify myself by discussing the details of what they produce to detest and to abolish this opinion, in short, to declare it not just false but heretical. They always shield themselves with a simulated religious zeal, and they also try to involve Holy Scripture and to make it somehow subservient to their insincere objectives; against the intention of Scripture and of the Holy Fathers (if I am not mistaken), they want to extend, not to say abuse, its authority, so that even for purely physical conclusions which are not matters of faith one must totally abandon the senses and demonstrative arguments in favor of any scriptural passage whose apparent words may contain a different indication.

Here I hope to demonstrate that I proceed with much more pious and religious zeal than they when I propose not that this book should not be condemned, but that it should not be condemned without understanding, examining, or even seeing it, as they would like. This is especially true since the author never treats of things pertaining to religion and faith, nor uses arguments dependent in any way on the authority of the Holy Scriptures, in which case he might have interpreted them incorrectly; instead, he always limits himself to physical conclusions pertaining to celestial motions, and he treats of them with astronomical and geometrical demonstrations based

---

9. Cardinal Nicolaus von Schoenberg (1472–1537), archbishop of Capua.
10. Tiedemann Giese (1480–1550), Polish friend of Copernicus.

above all on sense experience and very accurate observations. He proceeded in this manner not because he did not pay any attention to the passages of the Holy Scripture, but because he understood very well that [314] if his doctrine was demonstrated it could not contradict the properly interpreted Scripture. Hence, at the end of the dedication, speaking to the Supreme Pontiff, he says: "Perhaps there will be babblers who claim to be judges of astronomy although completely ignorant of the subject and, badly distorting some passage of Scripture to their purpose, will dare to find fault with my undertaking and censure it. I disregard them even to the extent of despising their criticism as unfounded. For it is not unknown that Lactantius, otherwise an illustrious writer but hardly an astronomer, speaks quite childishly about the earth's shape, when he mocks those who declared that the earth has the form of a globe. Hence scholars need not be surprised if any such persons will likewise ridicule me. Astronomy is written for astronomers. To them my work too will seem, unless I am mistaken, to make some contribution also to the Church, at the head of which Your Holiness now stands."[11]

Of this sort are also those who try to argue that this author should be condemned, without examining him; and to show that this is not only legitimate but a good thing, they use the authority of Scripture, of experts in sacred theology, and of Sacred Councils. I feel reverence for these authorities and hold them supreme, so that I should consider it most reckless to want to contradict them when they are used in accordance with the purpose of the Holy Church; similarly, I do not think it is wrong to speak out when it seems that someone, out of personal interest, wants to use them in a way different from the holiest intention of the Holy Church. Thus, while also believing that my sincerity will become self-evident, I declare not only that I intend to submit freely to the correction of any errors in matters pertaining to religion which I may have committed in this essay due to my ignorance, but I also declare that on these subjects I do not want to quarrel with anyone, even if the points are debatable. For my purpose is nothing but the following: if these reflections, which are far from my own profession, should contain (besides errors) anything that may lead someone to advance a useful caution for the Holy Church in her deliberations about the [315] Copernican system, then let it be accepted with whatever profit superiors will deem appropriate; if not, let my essay be torn up and burned, for I do not intend or pretend to gain from it any advantage that is not pious or Catholic. Moreover, although I have heard with my own ears many of the things which I mention, I freely grant to whoever said them that they did not say them, if they so wish, and I admit that I may have misunderstood them; thus what I answer should not apply to them, but to whoever holds that opinion.

---

11. Here quoted from Copernicus 1992, 5.

So the reason they advance to condemn the opinion of the earth's mobility and sun's stability is this: since in many places in the Holy Scripture one reads that the sun moves and the earth stands still, and since Scripture can never lie or err, it follows as a necessary consequence that the opinion of those who want to assert the sun to be motionless and the earth moving is erroneous and damnable.

[§2.2] The first thing to note about this argument is the following. It is most pious to say and most prudent to take for granted that Holy Scripture can never lie, as long as its true meaning has been grasped; but I do not think one can deny that this is frequently recondite and very different from what appears to be the literal meaning of the words. From this it follows that, if in interpreting it someone were to limit himself always to the pure literal meaning, and if the latter were wrong, then he could make Scripture appear to be full not only of contradictions and false propositions, but also of serious heresies and blasphemies; for one would have to attribute to God feet, hands, eyes, and bodily sensations, as well as human feelings like anger, contrition, and hatred, and such conditions as the forgetfulness of things past and the ignorance of future ones. Since these propositions dictated by the Holy Spirit were expressed by the sacred writers in such a way as to accommodate the capacities of the very unrefined and undisciplined masses, therefore for those who deserve to rise above the common people it is necessary that wise interpreters [316] formulate the true meaning and indicate the specific reasons why it is expressed by such words. This doctrine is so commonplace and so definite among all theologians that it would be superfluous to present any testimony for it.

From this I think one can very reasonably deduce that, whenever the same Holy Scripture has seen fit to assert any physical conclusion (especially on things that are abstruse and difficult to understand), it has followed the same rule, in order not to sow confusion into the minds of the common people and make them more obstinate against dogmas involving higher mysteries. In fact, as I said and as one can clearly see, for the sole purpose of accommodating popular understanding Scripture has not abstained from concealing the most important truths, attributing even to God characteristics that are contrary to or very far from His essence; given this, who will categorically maintain that in speaking incidentally of the earth, water, sun, or other created thing Scripture has set aside such regard and has chosen to limit itself rigorously to the literal and narrow meanings of the words? This would be especially implausible when mentioning features of these created things which are very remote from popular understanding, and which are not at all pertinent to the primary purpose of the Holy Writ, that is, to the worship of God and the salvation of souls.

Therefore, I think that in disputes about natural phenomena one must begin not with the authority of scriptural passages, but with sense experiences and necessary demonstrations. For the Holy Scripture and nature derive equally from the Godhead, the former as the dictation of the Holy Spirit and the latter as the most obedient executrix of God's orders; moreover, to accommodate the understanding of the common people it is appropriate for Scripture to say many things that are different (in appearance and in regard to the literal meaning of the words) from the absolute truth; on the other hand, nature is inexorable and immutable, never violates the terms of the laws imposed upon her, and does not care whether or not her recondite reasons and ways of operating are disclosed to human understanding; [317] but not every scriptural assertion is bound to obligations as severe as every natural phenomenon; finally, God reveals Himself to us no less excellently in the effects of nature than in the sacred words of Scripture, as Tertullian perhaps meant when he said, "We postulate that God ought first to be known by nature, and afterwards further known by doctrine—by nature through His works, by doctrine through official teaching" (*Against Marcion*, I.18);[12] and so it seems that a natural phenomenon which is placed before our eyes by sense experience or proved by necessary demonstrations should not be called into question, let alone condemned, on account of scriptural passages whose words appear to have a different meaning.

However, by this I do not wish to imply that one should not have the highest regard for passages of Holy Scripture; indeed, after becoming certain of some physical conclusions, we should use these as very appropriate aids to the correct interpretation of such Scriptures and to the investigation of the truths they must contain, for they are most true and agree with demonstrated truths. That is, I would say that the authority of Holy Scripture aims chiefly at persuading men about those articles and propositions which, surpassing all human reason, could not be discovered by scientific research or by any other means than through the mouth of the Holy Spirit himself. Moreover, even in regard to those propositions that are not articles of faith, the authority of the same Holy Writ should have priority over the authority of any human works composed not with the demonstrative method but with either pure narration or even probable reasons;[13] this principle should be considered appropriate and necessary inasmuch as divine wisdom surpasses all human judgment and speculation. However, I do not think one has to believe that the same God who has given us senses, language, and intellect would want to set aside the use of these and give us by other means the information we can acquire with them, so that we would deny our senses and reason even in the case of those physical conclusions which are

---

12. Tertullian 1972, 47; I have made some slight emendations to Evans's translation of this passage.
13. Here my translation of this sentence corrects the one given in Finocchiaro 1989, 94.

placed before our eyes and intellect by our sense experiences or by necessary demonstrations. This is especially implausible for those sciences discussed in Scripture to a very minor extent and [318] with disconnected statements; such is precisely the case of astronomy, so little of which is contained therein that one does not find there even the names of the planets, except for the sun, the moon, and only once or twice Venus, under the name of Morning Star. Thus, if the sacred authors had had in mind to teach people about the arrangement and motions of the heavenly bodies, and consequently to have us acquire this information from Holy Scripture, then, in my opinion, they would not have discussed so little of the topic—that is to say, almost nothing in comparison with the innumerable admirable conclusions which are contained and demonstrated in this science.

Indeed, it is the opinion of the holiest and most learned Fathers that the writers of Holy Scripture not only did not pretend to teach us about the structure and the motions of the heavens and of the stars, and their shape, size, and distance, but that they deliberately refrained from doing it, even though they knew all these things very well. For example, one reads the following words in Saint Augustine (*On the Literal Interpretation of Genesis*, book 2, chapter 9): "It is also customary to ask what one should believe about the shape and arrangement of heaven according to our Scriptures. In fact, many people argue a great deal about these things, which with greater prudence our authors omitted, which are of no use for eternal life to those who study them, and (what is worse) which take up a lot of time that ought to be spent on things pertaining to salvation. For what does it matter to me whether heaven, like a sphere, completely surrounds the earth, which is balanced at the center of the universe, or whether like a discus it covers the earth on one side from above? However, since the issue here is the authority of Scripture, let me repeat a point I have made more than once; that is, there is a danger that someone who does not understand the divine words may find in our books or infer from them something about these topics which seems to contradict received opinions, and then he might not believe at all the other useful things contained in its precepts, stories, and assertions; therefore, briefly, it should be said that our authors did know the truth about the shape of heaven, but that the Spirit of God, which was speaking through them, did not want to teach men these things which are of no use to salvation." (The same opinion is found in Peter Lombard's *Book of Sentences*.) The same contempt which the sacred writers had for the investigation of such properties of heavenly bodies is repeated by Saint Augustine in the following chapter 10, in regard to the question whether heaven should be thought to be in motion or standing still. He writes: "Some brethren have also advanced a question about the motion of heaven, [319] namely whether heaven moves or stands still. For if it moves, they say, how is it a firmament? But if it stands still, how do the stars which are thought to be fixed in it revolve from east to west, the northern ones completing shorter circuits near the pole, so that heaven seems to rotate like a sphere (if there is at the other end another pole invisible to us) or like a discus (if instead there is no other pole)? To them I answer that these things should be examined with very subtle and demanding arguments, to determine truly whether or not it is so; but I do not have the time to undertake and to pursue these investigations, nor should such time be available to those whom we desire to instruct for their salvation and for the needs and benefit of the Holy Church."

Let us now come down from these things to our particular point. We have seen that the Holy Spirit did not want to teach us whether heaven moves or stands still, nor whether its shape is spherical or like a discus or extended along a plane, nor whether the earth is located at its center or on one side. So it follows as a necessary consequence that the Holy Spirit also did not intend to teach us about other questions of the same kind and connected to those just mentioned in such a way that without knowing the truth about the former one cannot decide the latter, such as the question of the motion or rest of the earth or sun. But, if the Holy Spirit deliberately avoided teaching us such propositions, inasmuch as they are of no relevance to His intention (that is, to our salvation), how can one now say that to hold this rather than that proposition on this topic is so important that one is a principle of faith and the other erroneous? Thus, can an opinion be both heretical and irrelevant to the salvation of souls? Or can one say that the Holy Spirit chose not to teach us something relevant to our salvation? Here I would say what I heard from an ecclesiastical person in a very eminent position (Cardinal Baronio), namely that the intention of the Holy Spirit is to teach us how one goes to heaven and not how heaven goes.

But let us go back and examine the importance of necessary demonstrations and of sense experiences in conclusions about natural phenomena, and how much weight has been assigned to them by learned and holy theologians. Among hundreds of instances of such testimony we have the following. Near the beginning of his work *On Genesis*, Pererius asserts: [320] "In treating of Moses' doctrine, one must take diligent care to completely avoid holding and saying positively and categorically anything which contradicts the decisive observations and reasons of philosophy or other disciplines; in fact, since all truths always agree with one another, the truth of Holy Scripture cannot be contrary to the true reasons and observations of human doctrines." And in Saint Augustine (Letter to Marcellinus, section 7), one reads: "If, against the most manifest and reliable testimony of reason, anything be set up claiming to have the authority of the Holy Scriptures, he who does this does it through a misapprehension of what he has read and is setting up against the truth not the real meaning of Scripture, which he has failed to discover, but an opinion of his own; he alleges not what he has found in the Scriptures, but what he has found in himself as their interpreter."[14]

Because of this, and because (as we said above) two truths cannot contradict one another, the task of a wise interpreter is to strive to fathom the true meaning of the sacred texts; this will undoubtedly agree with those physical conclusions of which we are already certain and sure through clear observations or necessary demonstrations. Indeed, besides saying (as we have) that in many places Scripture is open to interpretations far removed from the literal meaning of the words, we should add that we cannot assert with certainty that all interpreters speak with divine inspiration, since if this were so then there would be no disagreement among them about the meaning of the same passages; therefore, I should think it would be very prudent not to allow anyone to commit and in a way oblige scriptural passages to have to maintain the truth of any physical conclusions whose contrary could ever be proved to us by the senses or demonstrative and necessary reasons. Indeed, who wants the human mind put to death? Who is going to claim that everything in the world which is observable and knowable has already been seen and discovered? Perhaps those who on other occasions admit, quite correctly, that the things we know are a very small part of the things we do not know? Indeed, we also have it from the mouth of the Holy Spirit that "God hath delivered the world to their consideration, so that man cannot find out the work which God hath made from the beginning to the end" (Ecclesiastes, chapter 3);[15] so one must not, in my opinion, contradict this statement and block the way of freedom of philosophizing about things [321] of the world and of nature, as if they had all already been discovered and disclosed with certainty.

Nor should it be considered rash to be dissatisfied with opinions which are almost universally accepted; nor should people become indignant if in a dispute about natural phenomena someone disagrees with the opinion they favor, especially in regard to problems which have been controversial for thousands of years among very great philosophers, such as the sun's rest and earth's motion. This opinion has been held by Pythagoras and his whole school, by Heraclides of Pontus, by Philolaus (teacher of Plato), and by Plato himself (as Aristotle and Plutarch mention); the latter writes in the "Life of Numa" that when Plato was old he said it was very absurd to believe otherwise. The same opinion was accepted by Aristarchus of Samos (as Archimedes tells us), by the mathematician Seleucus, by the philosopher Hicetas (according to Cicero[16]), and by many others; finally, it was amplified and confirmed with

---

14. Here quoted from Mourant 1964, 110.
15. Ecclesiastes 3:11 (Douay Version).
16. Cicero, *Academia*, II, 39, 123.

many observations and demonstrations by Nicolaus Copernicus. Furthermore, in the book *On Comets*, the very distinguished philosopher Seneca tells us that one should attempt to ascertain with the greatest diligence whether the daily rotation belongs to the heavens or to the earth.

Therefore, it would perhaps be wise and useful advice not to add without necessity to the articles pertaining to salvation and to the definition of the faith, against the firmness of which there is no danger that any valid and effective doctrine could ever emerge. If this is so, it would really cause confusion to add them upon request from persons about whom not only do we not know whether they speak with heavenly inspiration, but we clearly see that they are deficient in the intelligence necessary first to understand and then to criticize the demonstrations by which the most acute sciences proceed in confirming similar conclusions. However, if I may be allowed to state my opinion, I should say further that it would be more appropriate to the dignity and majesty of Holy Writ to take steps to insure that not every superficial and vulgar writer can lend credibility to his writings [322] (very often based on worthless fabrications) by sprinkling them with scriptural passages; these are often interpreted, or rather distorted, in ways which are as remote from the true intention of Scripture as they are ridiculously close to the aims of those who ostentatiously adorn their writings with them.

Many examples of such an abuse could be adduced, but I shall limit myself to two which are not far from these astronomical subjects. One of them consists of the writings that were published against the Medicean planets, which I recently discovered, and against the existence of which many passages of Holy Scripture were advanced; now that these planets can be seen by the whole world, I should very much like to hear in what new ways those same opponents interpret Scripture and excuse their blunder. The other example involves someone who has recently argued in print against astronomers and philosophers, to the effect that the moon does not receive its light from the sun but is itself luminous; ultimately he confirms, or rather convinces himself to be confirming, this fancy with various scriptural passages, which he thinks could not be accounted for if his opinion were not true and necessary. Nevertheless, it is as clear as sunlight that the moon is in itself dark.

It is thus obvious that, because these authors had not grasped the true meaning of Scripture, if they had commanded much authority they would have obliged it to compel others to hold as true conclusions repugnant to manifest reasons and to the senses. This is an abuse which I hope God will prevent from taking root or gaining influence, because it would in a short time require the prohibition of all ratiocinative sciences. In fact, the number of men ill-suited to understand adequately the Holy Scripture and the sciences is by nature much greater than the number of intelligent ones; thus the former, by superficially glancing through Scripture, would arrogate to themselves the authority of decreeing over all questions about nature in virtue of some word ill-understood by them and written by the sacred authors for some other purpose; nor could the small [323] number of the intelligent ones restrain the furious torrent of the others, who would find all the more followers, inasmuch as it is sweeter to be considered wise without study and labor than to wear oneself out unrelentingly in the pursuit of very arduous disciplines. However, we can render infinite thanks to the blessed God, whose benevolence frees us from this fear while it strips such persons of any authority. The deliberating, deciding, and decreeing about such important issues can be left to the excellent wisdom and goodness of very prudent Fathers and to the supreme authority of those who, guided by the Holy Spirit, can only behave in a holy manner and will not permit the irresponsibility of those others to gain influence.

These sorts of men are, in my opinion, those toward whom serious and saintly writers become angry, not without reason. For instance, referring to the Holy Scripture, Saint Jerome writes: "The chatty old woman, the doting old man, and the wordy sophist, one and all take in hand the Scriptures, rend them in pieces and teach them before they have learned them. Some with brows knit and bombastic words, balanced one against the other, philosophize concerning the sacred writings among weak women. Others—I blush to say it—learn of women what they are to teach men; and as if this were not enough, they boldly explain to others what they themselves by no means understand. I say nothing of persons who, like myself, have been familiar with secular literature before they have come to the study of the Holy Scriptures. Such men when they charm the popular ear by the finish of their style suppose every word they say to be a law of God. They do not deign to notice what prophets and apostles have intended but they adapt conflicting passages to suit their own meaning, as if it were a grand way of teaching—and not rather the faultiest of all—to misinterpret a writer's views and to force the Scriptures reluctantly to do their will" (Letter No. 53, to Paulinus).[17]

[§2.3] Among such lay writers should not be numbered some theologians whom I regard as men of profound learning and of the holiest life style, and whom I therefore hold in high esteem and reverence. However, I cannot deny having some qualms, which I consequently wish could be removed; for in disputes about natural phenomena they seem to claim the right to force others by means of the authority of Scripture to follow the opinion which they think is most in accordance with its statements, and at the same time they believe they are not obliged to [324] answer observations and reasons to the contrary. As an explanation and a justification of this opinion of theirs, they say that theology is the queen of all the sciences and hence must not in any way lower

---

17. Here quoted, with slight emendations, from Jerome 1893, 99. I have also corrected Galileo's reference, which he gives as letter no. 103.

herself to accommodate the principles of other less dignified disciplines subordinate to her; rather, these others must submit to her as to a supreme empress and change and revise their conclusions in accordance with theological rules and decrees; moreover, they add that whenever in the subordinate science there is a conclusion which is certain on the strength of demonstrations and observations, and which is repugnant to some other conclusion found in Scripture, the practitioners of that science must themselves undo their own demonstrations and disclose the fallacies of their own observations, without help from theologians and scriptural experts; for, as stated, it is not proper to the dignity of theology to stoop to the investigation of the fallacies in the subordinate sciences, but it is sufficient for it to determine the truth of a conclusion with absolute authority and with the certainty that it cannot err. Then they say that the physical conclusions in regard to which we must rely on Scripture, without glossing or interpreting it in nonliteral ways, are those of which Scripture always speaks in the same way, and which all the Holy Fathers accept and interpret with the same meaning. Now, I happen to have some specific ideas on these claims, and I shall propose them in order to receive the proper advice from whoever is more competent than I in these subjects; I always defer to their judgment.

To begin with, I think one may fall into something of an equivocation if one does not distinguish the senses in which sacred theology is preeminent and worthy of the title of queen. For it could be such insofar as whatever is taught in all the other sciences is found explained and demonstrated in it by means of more excellent methods and of more sublime principles, in the way that, for example, the rules for measuring fields and for accounting are better contained in Euclid's geometry and arithmetic than they are [325] in the practices of surveyors and accountants; or else insofar as the topic on which theology focuses surpasses in dignity all the other topics which are the subject of the other sciences, and also insofar as its teaching proceeds in more sublime ways. I do not believe that theologians who are acquainted with the other sciences can assert that theology deserves the royal title and authority in the first sense; I think no one will say that geometry, astronomy, music, and medicine are treated more excellently and exactly in the sacred books than in Archimedes, Ptolemy, Boethius, and Galen. So it seems that the royal preeminence belongs to it in the second sense, namely because of the eminence of the topic, and because of the admirable teaching of divine revelation in conclusions which could not be learned by men in any other way, and which concern chiefly the gaining of eternal bliss. So theology does deal with the loftiest divine contemplations, and for this it does occupy the royal throne and command the highest authority; and it does not come down to the lower and humbler speculations of the inferior sciences, but rather (as stated above) it does not bother with them, inasmuch as they are irrelevant to salvation. If all this is so, then officials and experts of theology should not arrogate to themselves the authority to issue decrees in the professions they neither exercise nor study; for this would be the same as if an absolute prince, knowing he had unlimited power to issue orders and to compel obedience, but being neither a physician nor an architect, wanted to direct medical treatment and the construction of buildings, resulting in serious danger to the life of the unfortunate sick and in the obvious collapse of structures.

Furthermore, to require astronomers to endeavor to protect themselves against their own observations and demonstrations, namely to show that these are nothing but fallacies and sophisms, is to demand they do the impossible; for [326] that would be to require that they not only should not see what they see and not understand what they understand, but also that in their research they should find the contrary of what they find. That is, before they can do this, they should be shown how to manage having the lower faculties of the soul direct the higher ones, so that the imagination and the will could and would believe the contrary of what the intellect thinks (I am always speaking of purely physical propositions which are not matters of faith, rather than of supernatural propositions which are articles of faith). I should like to ask these very prudent Fathers to agree to examine very diligently the difference between debatable and demonstrative doctrines. Keeping firmly in mind the compelling power of necessary deductions, they should come to see more clearly that it is not within the power of the practitioners of demonstrative sciences to change opinion at will, choosing now this now that one; that there is a great difference between giving orders to a mathematician or a philosopher and giving them to a merchant or a lawyer; and that demonstrated conclusions about natural and celestial phenomena cannot be changed with the same ease as opinions about what is or is not legitimate in a contract, in a rental, or in commerce.

This difference has been completely recognized by the holy and very learned Fathers, as shown by their having made [327] a great effort to confute many philosophical arguments or, to be more exact, fallacies, and may be explicitly read in some of them. In particular, we read the following words in Saint Augustine (*On the Literal Interpretation of Genesis*, book 1, chapter 21): "There should be no doubt about the following: whenever the experts of this world can truly demonstrate something about natural phenomena, we should show it not to be contrary to our Scriptures; but, whenever in their books they teach something contrary to the Holy Writ, we should without any doubt hold it to be most false, and also show this by any means we can; and in this way we should keep the faith of our Lord, in whom are hidden all the treasures of knowledge, in order not to be seduced by the verbosity of false philosophy or frightened by the superstition of fake religion."

These words imply, I think, the following doctrine: in the learned books of worldly authors are contained some propositions about nature which are truly demonstrated and others which are simply taught; in regard to the former, the task of wise theologians is to show that they are not contrary to Holy Scripture; as for the latter (which are taught but not demonstrated with necessity), if they contain anything contrary to the Holy Writ, then they must be considered indubitably false and must be demonstrated such by every possible means. So physical conclusions which have been truly demonstrated should not be given a lower place than scriptural passages, but rather one should clarify how such passages do not contradict those conclusions; therefore, before condemning a physical proposition, one must show that it is not conclusively demonstrated. Furthermore, it is much more reasonable and natural that this be done not by those who hold it to be true, but by those who regard it as false; for the fallacies of an argument can be found much more easily by those who regard it as false than by those who think it is true and conclusive, and indeed here it will happen that the more the followers of a given opinion thumb through books, examine the arguments, repeat the observations, and check the experiments, the more they will be testing [328] their belief.

In fact, Your Highness knows what happened to the late mathematician of the University of Pisa: in his old age he undertook an examination of Copernicus's doctrine with the hope of being able to refute it solidly, since he considered it false, even though he had never examined it; but it so happened that as soon as he understood its foundations, procedures, and demonstrations he became convinced of it, and he turned from opponent to very strong supporter. I could also name other mathematicians (e.g., Clavius) who, influenced by my recent discoveries, have admitted the necessity of changing the previous conception of the constitution of the world, since it can no longer stand up in any way.

It would be very easy to remove from the world the new opinion and doctrine if it were sufficient to shut the mouth of only one person; this is perhaps the belief of those who measure the judgments of others in terms of their own, and who thus think it is impossible that such an opinion can stand up and find followers. However, this business proceeds otherwise. For in order to accomplish that objective, it would be necessary not only to prohibit Copernicus's book and the writings of the other authors who follow the same doctrine, but also to ban all astronomical science completely; moreover, one would have to forbid men to look toward the heavens, so that they would not see that Mars and Venus are sometimes very close to and sometimes very far from the earth (the difference being that the latter sometimes appears forty times greater than at other times, and the former sixty times greater); nor should they be allowed to see the same Venus appear sometimes round and sometimes armed with very sharp horns,[18] and many other observable phenomena which can in no way be adapted to the Ptolemaic system but provide very strong arguments for Copernicanism. At the moment, because of many new [329] observations and because of many scholars' contributions to its study, one is discovering daily that Copernicus's position is truer and truer, and his doctrine firmer and firmer; so to prohibit Copernicus now, after being permitted for so many years when he was less widely followed and less well confirmed, would seem to me an encroachment on the truth and an attempt to step up its concealment and suppression in proportion to how much more it appears obvious and clear. Not to ban the whole book in its entirety, but to condemn as erroneous only this particular proposition, would cause greater harm to souls, if I am not mistaken; for it would expose them to the possibility of seeing the proof of a proposition which it would then be sinful to believe. To prohibit the entire science would be no different than to reject hundreds of statements from the Holy Writ, which teach us how the glory and the greatness of the supreme God are marvelously seen in all of His works and by divine grace are read in the open book of the heavens. Nor should anyone think that the reading of the very lofty words written on those pages is completed by merely seeing the sun and the stars give off light, rise, and set, which is as far as the eyes of animals and of common people reach; on the contrary, those pages contain such profound mysteries and such sublime concepts that the vigils, labors, and studies of hundreds of the sharpest minds in uninterrupted investigations for thousands of years have not yet completely fathomed them. Even idiots realize that what their eyes see when they look at the external appearance of a human body is very insignificant in comparison to the admirable contrivances found in it by a competent and diligent philosopher-anatomist when he investigates how so many muscles, tendons, nerves, and bones are used; when he examines the function of the heart and of the other principal organs; when he searches for the seat of the vital faculties; when he observes the wonderful structures of the senses; and, with no end to his astonishment and curiosity, when he studies the location of the imagination, of memory, [330] and of reason. Likewise, what the unaided sense of sight shows is almost nothing in comparison to the sublime marvels which the mind of intelligent investigators reveals in the heavens through long and accurate observations. This is all I can think of in regard to this particular point.

[§2.4] Let us now examine their other argument: that physical propositions concerning which Scripture always says the same thing, and which all the Fathers unanimously accept in the same sense, should be understood in accordance with the literal meaning of the words, without glosses or interpretations,

---

18. Both the variation in apparent magnitude of Mars and Venus, and the phases of Venus, had been previously undetected, but they became observable with the telescope soon after the publication of *The Sidereal Messenger*.

and should be accepted and held as most true; and that, since the sun's motion and earth's rest is a proposition of this sort, consequently it is an article of faith to hold it as true, and the contrary opinion is erroneous.

Here it should be noticed, first, that some physical propositions are of a type such that by any human speculation and reasoning one can only attain a probable opinion and a verisimilar conjecture about them, rather than a certain and demonstrated science; an example is whether the stars are animate. Others are of a type such that either one has, or one may firmly believe that it is possible to have, complete certainty on the basis of experiments, long observations, and necessary demonstrations; examples are whether or not the earth and the sun move, and whether or not the earth is spherical. As for the first type, I have no doubt at all that, where human reason cannot reach, and where consequently one cannot have a science, but only opinion and faith, it is appropriate piously to conform absolutely to the literal meaning of Scripture. In regard to the others, however, I should think, as stated above, that it would be proper to ascertain the facts first, so that they could guide us in finding the true meaning of Scripture; this would be found to agree absolutely with demonstrated facts, even though prima facie the words would sound otherwise, since two truths can never contradict each other.

This doctrine seems to me very [331] correct and certain, inasmuch as I find it exactly written in Saint Augustine. At one point he discusses the shape of heaven and what one should believe it to be, given that what astronomers affirm seems to be contrary to Scripture, since the former consider it round while the latter calls it stretched out like hide.[19] He decides one should not have the slightest worry that Scripture may contradict astronomers: one should accept its authority if what they say is false and based only on conjecture typical of human weakness; however, if what they say is proved with indubitable reasons, this Holy Father does not say that astronomers themselves be ordered to refute their demonstrations and declare their conclusion false, but he says one must show that what Scripture asserts about the hide is not contrary to those true demonstrations. Here are his words (*On the Literal Interpretation of Genesis*, book 2, chapter 9): "However, someone asks how what is written in our books, 'Who stretchest out the heavens like a hide,' does not contradict those who attribute to heaven the shape of a sphere. Now, if what they say is false, let it contradict them by all means, for the truth lies in what is said by divine authority rather than what is conjectured by human weakness. But if, by chance, they can support it with such evidence that one cannot doubt it,

---

19. On the issue mentioned here and discussed in the next several sentences, see Psalms 103:2 (Douay), corresponding to Psalms 104:2 (King James Version), as well as Isaiah 40:22; cf. Russo (1968, 346, nn. 1 and 2), and Finocchiaro (1989, 104–5, 339 nn. 37 and 37).

then we have to demonstrate that what our books say about the hide is not contrary to those true reasons." Then he goes on to warn us that we must not be less careful in reconciling a scriptural passage with a demonstrated physical proposition than with another scriptural passage that may appear contrary. Indeed I think the caution of this saint deserves to be admired and emulated; for even in the case of obscure conclusions concerning which one cannot be sure whether they can be the subject of a science based on human demonstrations, he is very careful in declaring what one should believe. This can be seen from what he writes at the end of the second book of *On the Literal Interpretation of Genesis*, when discussing whether stars should be considered animate: "Although at present this cannot be easily known, nevertheless I think that in the course of examining Scripture one may find more appropriate passages whereby we would be entitled, if not to prove something for certain, at least to believe something on this topic based on the words of the sacred authority. Now then, always practicing a pious and serious moderation, we ought not to believe anything lightly about an obscure subject, lest [332] we reject (out of love for our error) something which later may be truly shown not to be in any way contrary to the holy books of either the Old or New Testament."

From this and other places it seems to me, if I am not mistaken, the intention of the Holy Fathers is that in questions about natural phenomena which do not involve articles of faith one must first consider whether they are demonstrated with certainty or known by sense experience, or whether it is possible to have such knowledge and demonstration. When one is in possession of this, since it too is a gift from God, one must apply it to the investigation of the true meanings of the Holy Writ at those places which apparently seem to read differently. These meanings will undoubtedly be grasped by wise theologians, along with the reasons why the Holy Spirit has sometimes wanted to hide them under words with a different literal meaning, whether in order to test us or for some other reason unknown to me.

Returning to the preceding argument, if we keep in mind the primary aim of the Holy Writ, I do not think that its always saying the same thing should make us disregard this rule; for if to accommodate popular understanding Scripture finds it necessary once to express a proposition with words whose meaning differs from the essence of the proposition, why should it not follow the same practice for the same reason every time it has to say the same thing? On the contrary, I think that to do otherwise would increase popular confusion and diminish the propensity to believe on the part of the people. Furthermore, in regard to the rest or motion of the sun and of the earth, experience clearly shows that to accommodate popular understanding it is indeed necessary to assert what the words of Scripture say; for even in our age when people are more refined, they are kept in the same opinion by reasons which, when carefully examined and pondered, will be found to be most frivolous and by observations which are either completely false or totally irrelevant; nor can one try to move them since they are not capable of understanding the contrary reasons, which are dependent on extremely delicate observations and on subtle demonstrations [333] supported by abstractions whose understanding requires a very vivid imagination. Therefore, even if the sun's rest and the earth's motion were more than certain and demonstrated among the experts, it would still be necessary to utter the contrary in order to maintain credibility with large numbers of people; for among a thousand laymen who might be asked about these details, perhaps not even one will be found who would not answer that he firmly believes that the sun moves and the earth stands still. However, no one should take this very common popular consensus as an argument for the truth of what is being asserted; for if we ask the same men about the reasons and motives why they believe that way, and if on the other hand we listen to the observations and demonstrations which induce those other few to believe the opposite, we shall find that the latter are convinced by very solid reasons and the former by the simplest appearances and by empty and ridiculous considerations.

It is therefore clear that it was necessary to attribute motion to the sun and rest to the earth in order not to confuse the meager understanding of the people, and not to make them obstinately reluctant to give assent to the principal dogmas which are absolutely articles of faith; but if it was necessary to do this, it is no wonder that this was most prudently done in divine Scripture. Indeed I shall say further that it was not only respect for popular inability, but also the current opinion of those times, that made the sacred writers accommodate themselves to received usage rather than to the essence of the matter in regard to subjects which are not necessary for eternal bliss.

In fact, speaking of this Saint Jerome writes: "As if in the Holy Scriptures many things were not said in accordance with the opinion of the time when the facts are being reported, and not in accordance with the truth of the matter" (Commentary on Jeremiah, chapter 28). Elsewhere the same saint says: "In Scripture it is customary for the historian to report many opinions as they were accepted by everyone at that time" (Commentary on Matthew, chapter 13[20]). Finally, on the words in chapter 27 of Job, "He stretched out the north [334] over the empty space, and hangeth the earth upon nothing,"[21] Saint Thomas notes that Scripture calls empty and nothing the space which embraces and surrounds the earth, and which we know is not empty but full of air; nevertheless, he says that Scripture calls it empty and nothing in order to accommodate the belief of the people, who think there is nothing in this

---

20. Here Galileo's reference is inaccurate and should read "chapter 14 of book 2," as Damanti (2010, 218) points out.
21. Job 26:7 (Douay).

space. Here are Saint Thomas's words: "The upper hemisphere of the heavens seems to us nothing but a space full of air, though common people consider it empty; thus, it speaks in accordance with the judgment of common people, as is the custom in Holy Scripture."

Now from this I think one can obviously argue that analogously the Holy Scripture had a much greater reason to call the sun moving and the earth motionless. For if we test the understanding of common people, we shall find them much more incapable of becoming convinced of the sun's rest and earth's motion than of the fact that the space surrounding us is full of air; therefore, if the sacred authors refrained from attempting to persuade the people about this point, which was not that difficult for their understanding, it seems very reasonable to think that they followed the same style in regard to other propositions which are much more recondite.

Indeed, Copernicus himself knew how much our imagination is dominated by an old habit and by a way of conceiving things which is already familiar to us since infancy, and so he did not want to increase the confusion and difficulty of his abstraction. Thus, after first demonstrating that the motions which appear to us as belonging to the sun or the firmament [335] really belong to the earth, then, in the process of compiling their tables and applying them in practice, he speaks of them as belonging to the sun and to the part of heaven above the planets; for example, he speaks of the rising and setting of the sun and of the stars, of changes in the obliquity of the zodiac and in the equinoctial points, of the mean motion and the anomaly and the prosthaphaeresis[22] of the sun, and other similar things, which really belong to the earth. We call facts these things which appear to us as facts because, being attached to the earth, we are part of all its motions, and consequently we cannot directly detect these things in it but find it useful to consider it in relation to the heavenly bodies in which they appear to us. Therefore, note how appropriate it is to accommodate our usual manner of thinking.

Next consider the principle that the collective consensus of the Fathers, when they all accept in the same sense a physical proposition from Scripture, should authenticate it in such a way that it becomes an article of faith to hold it. I should think that at most this ought to apply only to those conclusions which the Fathers discussed and inspected with great diligence and debated on both sides of the issue, and for which then they all agreed to reject one side and hold the other. However, the earth's motion and sun's rest are not of this sort, given that in those times this opinion was totally forgotten and far from academic dispute, and was not examined, let alone followed, by anyone;

---

22. In mathematical astronomy, prosthaphaeresis is "the correction necessary to find the 'true', i.e., actual apparent, place of a planet, etc. from the mean place" (*Oxford English Dictionary*).

thus one may believe that the Fathers did not even think of discussing it, since the scriptural passages, their own opinion, and popular consensus were all in agreement, and no [336] contradiction by anyone was heard. Therefore, it is not enough to say that all the Fathers accept the earth's rest, etc., and so it is an article of faith to hold it; rather one would have to prove that they condemned the contrary opinion. For I can always say that their failure to reflect upon it and to discuss it made them leave it and allow it as the current opinion, but not as something resolved and established. I think I can say this with very good reason: for either the Fathers reflected upon this conclusion as if it were controversial, or they did not; if not, then they could not have decided anything about it, even in their minds, nor should their failure oblige us to accept those principles which they did not, even in intention, impose; whereas if they examined it with care, then they would have condemned it had they judged it to be erroneous; but there is no record of their having done this. Indeed, after some theologians began to examine it, one sees that they did not deem it to be erroneous, as one can read in Diego de Zúñiga's *Commentaries on Job*, in regard to the words "Who shaketh the earth out of her place, etc." in chapter 9, verse 6; he discusses the Copernican position at length and concludes that the earth's motion is not against Scripture.

Furthermore, I would have doubts about the truth of this prescription, namely whether it is true that the Church obliges one to hold as articles of faith such conclusions about natural phenomena, which are characterized only by the unanimous interpretation of all the Fathers. I believe it may be that those who think in this manner may want to amplify the decrees of the Councils in favor of their own opinion. For I do not see that in this regard they prohibit anything but tampering, in ways contrary to the interpretation of the Holy Church or of the collective consensus of the Fathers, with those propositions which are articles of faith, or which involve morals and pertain [337] to edification according to Christian doctrine; so speaks the Fourth Session of the Council of Trent. However, the motion or rest of the earth or the sun are not articles of faith and are not against morals; nor does anyone want to twist scriptural passages to contradict the Holy Church or the Fathers. Indeed, those who put forth this doctrine have never used scriptural passages, for it always remains the prerogative of serious and wise theologians to interpret the said passages in accordance with their true meaning. Moreover, it is very obvious that the decrees of the Councils agree with the Holy Fathers in regard to these details; for they are very far from wanting to accept as articles of faith similar physical conclusions or to reject as erroneous the contrary opinions, so much so that they prefer to pay attention to the primary intention of the Holy Church and consider it useless to spend time trying to ascertain those conclusions. Let me tell Your Most Serene Highness what Saint Augustine (*On the Literal Interpretation of Genesis*, book 2, chapter 10) answers to those brethren who ask whether it is true that the heavens move or stand still: "To them I answer that these things should be examined with very subtle and demanding arguments, to determine truly whether or not it is so; but I do not have the time to undertake and to pursue these investigations, nor should such time be available to those whom we desire to instruct for their salvation and for the needs and benefit of the Holy Church."

However, suppose one were to decide that, even in the case of propositions about natural phenomena, they should be condemned or accepted on the basis of scriptural passages which are unanimously interpreted in the same way by all the Fathers; even then I do not see that this rule would apply in our case, given that one can read in the Fathers different interpretations of the same passages. For example, Dionysius the Areopagite says that it was not the sun but the Prime Mobile which stopped;[23] Saint Augustine thinks the same thing, namely that all heavenly bodies stopped; and the Bishop of Avila[24] is of the same opinion. Moreover, among the Jewish authors whom Josephus endorses, some thought that the sun did not really stop, but that it appeared so for the short time during which the Israelites defeated their enemies. Similarly, in the miracle at the time of Hezekiah,[25] Paul of Burgos thinks that it did not take place in the sun but in the clock. [338] At any rate, I shall demonstrate further below that, regardless of the world system one assumes, it is in fact necessary to gloss and to interpret the words of the text in Joshua.

[§2.5] Finally, let us grant these gentlemen more than they ask—namely, let us submit entirely to the opinion of wise theologians. Since this particular determination was not made by the ancient Fathers, it could be made by the wise ones of our age. The controversy concerns questions of natural phenomena and dilemmas whose answers are necessary and cannot be otherwise than in one of the two controversial ways; so they should first hear the experiments, observations, reasons, and demonstrations of philosophers and astronomers on both sides of the question, and then they would be able to determine with certainty whatever divine inspiration will communicate to them. No one should hope or fear that they would reach such an important decision without inspecting and discussing very minutely all the reasons for one side and for the other, and without ascertaining the facts: this cannot be hoped for by those who would pay no attention to risking the majesty and dignity of the Holy Writ to support their self-righteous creations; nor is this to be feared by those who seek nothing but the examination of the foundations of this doctrine with the greatest care, and who do this only out of zeal for the truth and

---

23. Cf. Joshua 10:12–13, further discussed at great length a few pages below.
24. Alfonso Tostado (1400–1455), professor of theology and philosophy at the University of Salamanca (Spain).
25. Isaiah 38:8.

for the majesty, dignity, and authority of the Holy Writ, which every Christian must strive to uphold. No one can fail to see that this dignity is desired and upheld with much greater zeal by one group than by the other—by those who submit in every way to the Holy Church and who do not ask for the prohibition of this or that opinion, but only that they be allowed to present things whereby she could more reliably be sure of making the safest choice; and not by those who, blinded by their own interests or incited by malicious suggestions, preach that she immediately flash the sword since she has the power to do it, without considering that it is not always useful to do all that one can do.

This opinion was not held by the holiest Fathers. Indeed, they knew how harmful and how contrary to the primary function of the Catholic Church it would be to want to use scriptural passages to establish conclusions about nature, when by means of observations and of necessary demonstrations one could at some point demonstrate the contrary of what [339] the words literally say; thus, not only were they very circumspect, but they left precepts for the edification of others. From Saint Augustine, *On the Literal Interpretation of Genesis*, book 1, chapters 18 and 19,[26] we have the following: "In obscure subjects very far removed from our eyes, it may happen that even in the divine writings we read things that can be interpreted in different ways by different people, all consistent with the faith we have; in such a case, let us not rush into any one of these interpretations with such precipitous commitment that we are ruined if it is rightly undermined by a more diligent and truthful investigation; such recklessness would mean that we were struggling for our opinions and not for those of Scripture, and that we wanted to make scriptural opinion conform to ours, when we ought to want to make ours conform to that of Scripture." A little further, to teach us how no proposition can be against the faith unless it is first shown to be false, he adds: "It is not against the faith as long as it is not refuted by an unquestionable truth; if this happens, then it was not contained in the divine Scripture but originated from human ignorance." From this one sees the falsehood of any meanings given to scriptural passages which do not agree with demonstrated truths; and so one must search for the correct meaning of Scripture with the help of demonstrated truth, rather than taking the literal meaning of the words, which may seem to be the truth to our weak understanding, and trying somehow to force nature and to deny observations and necessary demonstrations.

Your Highness should also note with how much circumspection this very holy man proceeds before deciding to assert that some scriptural interpretation is so certain and sure that there is no fear of encountering disturbing difficulties; not satisfied with just any scriptural meaning which might agree

---

26. Of the several quotations in this paragraph and the next, the next is the only one that comes from chapter 18; the others six quotations all come from chapter 19.

with some demonstration, he adds: "But if this were proved to be true by
an unquestionable argument, it would be still uncertain whether by these
words the writer of the holy books meant this or something else no less true;
for if the rest of the context of the passage showed that he did not intend
this, then what he did intend would not thereby be falsified but would still
be true and more beneficial to know." Now, what increases our amazement
about the circumspection with which this author proceeds is the fact that he
is still not completely sure upon seeing that demonstrative reasons, as well as
the literal scriptural meaning and the preceding and subsequent text, [340]
all point in the same direction, and so he adds the following words: "If the
context of Scripture did not disprove that the writer meant this, one could
still ask whether he might not have meant the other." Still he does not decide
to accept this meaning or exclude that one, but rather he does not think
he can ever be sufficiently cautious, and so he continues: "If we found that he
could have meant the other, then it would be uncertain which of the two he
intended; and if both interpretations were supported by solid documentation,
it would not be implausible to believe that he meant both." Next, he seems
to want to give the rationale for his procedure by showing to us the dangers
to which certain people would expose themselves, Scripture, and the Church;
these are people who, concerned more with the preservation of their own
errors than with the dignity of Scripture, would want to extend its authority
beyond the limits which it prescribes for itself. And so he adds the following
words, which by themselves should suffice to repress and to temper the excessive license which some people arrogantly take: "In fact, it often happens that
even a non-Christian has views based on very conclusive reasons or observations about the earth, heaven, the other elements of this world, the motion
and revolutions or the size and distances of the stars, the eclipses of the sun
and moon, the cycles of years and epochs, the nature of animals, of plants, of
rocks, and similar things. Now, it is very scandalous, as well as harmful and
to be avoided at all costs, that any infidel should hear a Christian speak about
these things as if he were doing so in accordance with the Christian Scriptures and should see him err so deliriously as to be forced into laughter. The
distressing thing is not so much that an erring man should be laughed at, but
that our authors should be thought by outsiders to believe such things, and
should be criticized and rejected as ignorant, to the great detriment of those
whose salvation we care about. For how can they believe our books in regard
to the resurrection of the dead, the hope of eternal life, and the kingdom of
heaven, when they catch a Christian committing an error about something
they know very well, when they declare false his opinion taken from those
books, and when they find these full of fallacies in regard to things they have
already been able to observe or to establish by unquestionable argument?"
Finally, we can see how offended are the truly wise and prudent Fathers by

these people who, in order to support propositions they do not [341] understand, constrain scriptural passages in certain ways and then compound their
first error by producing other passages which they understand even less than
the former ones. This is explained by the same saint with the following words:
"It is impossible to express sufficiently well how much harm and sorrow those
who are reckless and presumptuous cause to prudent brethren. This happens
when they begin to be rebuked and refuted for their distorted and false opinions by those who do not accept the authority of our books, and so they put
forth those same books to prove and to defend what they had said with very
superficial recklessness and very obvious falsity, and they even quote many
of their passages from memory, considering them supporting testimony, but
without understanding either what they say or what they are talking about."

To this type belong, I think, those who will not or cannot understand the
demonstrations and the observations with which the originator and the followers of this position confirm it, and who thus are concerned with putting
forth Scripture. They do not notice that the more scriptural passages they
produce, and the more they persist in claiming that these are very clear and
not susceptible to other meanings besides what they advance, the greater the
harm resulting to the dignity of Scripture if later the truth were known to be
clearly contrary and were to cause confusion (especially if these people's judgment had much authority in the first place). There would be harm and confusion at least among those who are separated from the Holy Church, toward
whom she is nevertheless very zealous like a mother who wants to be able to
hold them on her lap. Your Highness can therefore see how inappropriate is
the procedure of those who, in disputes about nature, as a first step advance
arguments based on scriptural passages, especially when very often they do not
adequately understand these.

However, if these people truly feel and fully believe they have the true
meaning of some particular scriptural passage, it would have to follow necessarily that they are also sure of possessing the absolute truth about the physical
conclusion they intend to discuss and, at the same time, that they know they
have a very great advantage over the opponent, who has to defend the false
side; for whoever is supporting the truth can have many sense experiences and
many necessary demonstrations on his side, [342] whereas the opponent cannot use anything but deceptive presentations, paralogisms, and fallacies. Now,
if they know that by staying within the limits of the physical subject of discussion and using only philosophical weapons, they are in any case so superior to
the opponent, why is it that when they come to the debate they immediately
seize an irresistible and fearful weapon, so that their opponent is frightened at
its mere sight? To tell the truth, I believe they are the ones who are frightened; feeling unable to resist the opponent's assaults, they try to find a way of
repelling him by forbidding him to use the reason which he received through

the Divine Goodness, and by abusing the very proper authority of the Holy Scripture, which (when adequately understood and used) can never conflict with clear observation and necessary demonstrations, as all theologians agree.[27] However, the fact that these people take refuge in Scripture, to cover up their inability to understand and to answer the contrary arguments, should be of no advantage to them, if I am not mistaken, since till now such an opinion has never been condemned by the Holy Church. Therefore, if they wanted to proceed with sincerity, they could remain silent and admit their inability to discuss similar subjects; or else they could first reflect that it is not within their power, nor within that of anyone but the Supreme Pontiff and the sacred Councils, to declare a proposition erroneous, but that they are free to discuss whether it is false; then, understanding that it is impossible for a proposition to be both true and heretical, they should focus on the issue which more concerns them, namely on demonstrating its falsity; if they were to discover this falsity, then either it would no longer be necessary to prohibit it because no one would follow it, or its prohibition would be safe and without the risk of any scandal.

Thus, let these people apply themselves to refuting the arguments of Copernicus and of the others, and let them leave its condemnation as erroneous and heretical to the proper authorities; but let them not hope that the very cautious and very wise Fathers and the Infallible One with his absolute wisdom are about to make rash decisions like those into which they would be rushed by their special interests and feelings. [343] For in regard to these and other similar propositions which do not directly involve the faith, no one can doubt that the Supreme Pontiff always has the absolute power of permitting or condemning them; however, no creature has the power of making them be true or false, contrary to what they happen to be by nature and de facto. So it seems more advisable to first become sure about the necessary and immutable truth of the matter, over which no one has control, than to condemn one side when such certainty is lacking; this would imply a loss of freedom of decision and of choice insofar as it would give necessity to things which are presently indifferent, free, and dependent on the will of the supreme authority. In short, if it is inconceivable that a proposition should be declared heretical when one thinks that it may be true, it should be futile for someone to try to bring about the condemnation of the earth's motion and sun's rest unless he first shows it to be impossible and false.

[§2.6] There remains one last thing for us to examine: to what extent it is true that the Joshua passage[28] can be taken without altering the literal meaning

---

27. Here I have improved the translation of this sentence found in Finocchiaro 1989, 113.

28. Joshua 10:12–13, which I quote in the Introduction (§0.3), above.

of the words and how it can be that, when the sun obeyed Joshua's order to stop, from this it followed that the day was prolonged by a large amount.

Given the heavenly motions in accordance with the Ptolemaic system, this is something which in no way can happen. For the sun's motion along the ecliptic takes place in the order of the signs of the zodiac, which is from west to east; this is contrary to the motion of the Prime Mobile from east to west, which is what causes day and night; therefore, it is clear that if the sun stops its own true motion, the day becomes shorter and not longer and that, on the contrary, the way to prolong it would be to speed up the sun's motion; thus, to make the sun stay for some time at the same place above the horizon, without going down toward the west, [344] it would be necessary to accelerate its motion so as to equal the motion of the Prime Mobile, which would be to accelerate it to about three hundred and sixty times its usual motion. Hence, if Joshua had wanted his words taken in their literal and most proper meaning, he would have told the sun to accelerate its motion by an amount such that, when carried along by the Prime Mobile, it would not be made to set; but his words were being heard by people who perhaps had no other knowledge of heavenly motions except for the greatest and most common one from east to west; thus he adapted himself to their knowledge and spoke in accordance with their understanding, because he did not want to teach them about the structure of the spheres but to make them understand the greatness of the miracle of the prolongation of the day.

Perhaps it was this consideration that first led Dionysius the Areopagite (in the Letter to Polycarpus) to say that in this miracle the Prime Mobile stopped and, as a consequence of its stopping, all other celestial spheres stopped. The same opinion is held by Saint Augustine himself (in book 2 of *On the Miracles of the Holy Scripture*), and the Bishop of Avila supports it at length (in questions 22 and 24 of his commentary on chapter 10 of Joshua). Indeed one sees that Joshua himself intended to stop the whole system of celestial spheres, from his giving the order also to the moon, even though it has nothing to do with the prolongation of the day; in the injunction given to the moon one must include the orbs of the other planets, which are not mentioned here, as they are not in the rest of the Holy Scripture, since its intention has never been to teach us the astronomical sciences.

I think therefore, if I am not mistaken, that one can clearly see that, given the Ptolemaic system, it is necessary to interpret the words in a way different from their literal meaning. Guided by Saint Augustine's very useful prescriptions, I should say that the best nonliteral interpretation is not necessarily this, if anyone can find another which is perhaps better and more suitable. So now I want to examine whether the same miracle could be understood in a way more in accordance with what we read in Joshua, if to the Copernican system we add [345] another discovery which I recently made about the solar body.

However, I continue to speak with the same reservations—to the effect that I am not so enamored with my own opinions as to want to place them ahead of those of others; nor do I believe it is impossible to put forth interpretations which are better and more in accordance with the Holy Writ.

Let us first assume, in accordance with the opinion of the above-mentioned authors, that in the Joshua miracle the whole system of heavenly motions was stopped, so that the stopping of only one would not introduce unnecessarily universal confusion and great turmoil in the whole order of nature. Second, I think that although the solar body does not move from the same place, it turns on itself, completing an entire rotation in about one month, as I feel I have conclusively demonstrated in my *Sunspot Letters*; this motion is sensibly seen to be inclined southward in the upper part of the globe, and thus to tilt northward in the lower part, precisely in the same manner as the revolutions of all planetary orbs. Third, the sun may be regarded as a noble body, and it is the source of light illuminating not only the moon and the earth but also all the other planets, which are in themselves equally dark; having conclusively demonstrated this, I do not think it would be far from correct philosophizing to say that, insofar as it is the greatest minister of nature and, in a way, the heart and soul of the world, it transmits to the surrounding bodies not only light, but also (by turning on itself) motion; thus, just as all motion of the limbs of an animal would cease if the motion of its heart were to cease, in the same way if the sun's rotation stopped then all planetary revolutions would also stop.

Now, concerning the admirable power and strength of the sun I could quote the supporting statements of many serious writers, but I want to restrict myself to just one passage from the book *The Divine Names* by the Blessed Dionysius the Areopagite. He writes this about the sun: "Light also gathers and attracts to itself all things that are seen, that move, that are illuminated, that are heated, and in a word that are surrounded by its splendor. Thus the sun is called Helios because [346] it collects and gathers all things that are dispersed." And a little below that he again writes about the sun: "If in fact this sun, which we see and which (despite the multitude and dissimilarity of the essences and qualities of observed things) is nevertheless one, spreads its light equally and renews, nourishes, preserves, perfects, divides, joins, warms up, fertilizes, increases, changes, strengthens, produces, moves, and vitalizes all things; and if everything in this universe in accordance with its own power partakes of one and the same sun and contains within itself an equal anticipation of the causes of the many things which are shared; then certainly all the more reason, etc."

Therefore, given that the sun is both the source of light and the origin of motion, and given that God wanted the whole world system to remain motionless for several hours as a result of Joshua's order, it was sufficient to stop the sun, and then its immobility stopped all the other turnings, so that the earth as well as the moon and the sun (and all the other planets) remained in the same arrangement; and during that whole time the night did not approach, and the day miraculously got longer. In this manner, by stopping the sun, and without changing or upsetting at all the way the other stars appear or their mutual arrangement, the day on the earth could have been lengthened in perfect accord with the literal meaning of the sacred text.

Furthermore, what deserves special appreciation, if I am not mistaken, is that with the Copernican system one can very clearly and very easily give a literal meaning to another detail which one reads about the same miracle; that is, that the sun stopped in the middle of heaven. Serious theologians have raised a difficulty about this passage: it seems very probable that, when Joshua asked for the prolongation of the day, the sun was close to setting and not at the meridian; for it was then about the time of the summer solstice, and consequently the days were very long, so that if the sun had been at the meridian then it does not seem likely that it would have been necessary to pray for a lengthening of the day in order to win a battle, since the still remaining time of seven hours or more could very well have been sufficient. Motivated by this argument, very serious theologians have held that the sun really was close to setting; [347] this is also what the words "Sun, stand thou still" seem to say, because if it had been at the meridian, then either there would have been no need to seek a miracle or it would have been sufficient to pray merely for some slowing down. This opinion is held by Caietanus, and it is also accepted by Magalhães, who confirms it by saying that on the same day, before the order to the sun, Joshua had done so many other things that it was impossible to complete them in half a day; thus they really resort to interpreting the words "in the midst of heaven" somewhat implausibly, saying they mean the same as that the sun stopped while it was in our hemisphere, namely above the horizon. We can remove this and every other implausibility, if I am not mistaken, by placing the sun, as the Copernican system does and as it is most necessary to do, in the middle, namely at the center of the heavenly orbs and of the planetary revolutions; for at any hour of the day, whether at noon or in the afternoon, the day would have been lengthened and all heavenly turnings stopped by the sun stopping in the middle of the heavens, namely at the center of the heavens, where it is located. Furthermore, this interpretation agrees all the more with the literal meaning inasmuch as, if one wanted to claim that the sun's stopping occurred at the noon hour, then the proper expression to use would have been to say that it "stood still at the meridian point," or "at the meridian circle," and not "in the midst of heaven"; in fact, for a spherical body such as heaven, the middle is really and only the center.

As for other scriptural passages which seem to contradict this position, I have no doubt that, if it were known to be true and demonstrated, those same theologians who consider such passages incapable of being interpreted

consistently with it (as long as they regard it as false) would find highly con-
genial interpretations for them; this would be especially true if they were to
add some knowledge of the astronomical sciences to their expertise about
Holy Writ. Just as now, when they consider it false, they think that whenever they read Scripture they only find statements repugnant to it, so if they
thought otherwise they would perchance find an equal number of passages
agreeing with it. Then perhaps they would judge [348] it very appropriate for
the Holy Church to tell us that God placed the sun at the center of heaven,
and that therefore He brings about the ordered motions of the moon and the
other wandering stars by making it turn around itself like a wheel, given that
she sings:

> Most holy Lord and God of heaven,
> Who to the glowing sky hast given
> The fires that in the east are born
> With gradual splendours of the morn;
> Who, on the fourth day, didst reveal
> The sun's enkindled flaming wheel,
> Didst set the moon her ordered ways,
> And stars their ever-winding maze.[29]

They could also say that the word firmament is *literally* very appropriate
for the stellar sphere and everything above the planetary orbs, which is totally
still and motionless according to this arrangement. Similarly, if the earth were
rotating, then, where one reads "He had not yet made the earth, nor the riv-
ers, nor the poles of the terrestrial globe,"[30] one could understand its poles
literally; for there would be no point in attributing these poles to the terrestrial
globe if it did not have to turn around them.

---

29. Here quoted from *The English Hymnal with Tunes* (London: Oxford University
Press, 1933), p. 89.
30. Cf. Proverbs 8:26; I have translated Galileo's Latin quotation literally in order to
appreciate his point.

CHAPTER 2

Epistemological Issues:
Hypothesis vs. Reality

§3. Bellarmine's Letter to Foscarini (12 April 1615)[1]

[171] I have read with interest the letter in Italian and the essay in Latin which Your Paternity sent me; I thank you for the one and for the other, and confess that they are all full of intelligence and erudition. You ask for my opinion, and so I shall give it to you, but very briefly, since now you have little time for reading and I for writing.

First, I say that it seems to me that Your Paternity and Mr. Galileo are proceeding prudently by limiting yourselves to speaking suppositionally and not absolutely, as I have always believed that Copernicus spoke. For there is no danger in saying that, by assuming the earth moves and the sun stands still, one saves all the appearances better than by postulating eccentrics and epicycles; and that is sufficient for the mathematician. However, it is different to want to affirm that in reality the sun is at the center of the world and only turns on itself without moving from east to west, and the earth is in the third heaven[2] and revolves with great speed around the sun; this is a very dangerous thing, likely not only to irritate all scholastic philosophers and theologians, but also to harm the Holy Faith by rendering Holy Scripture false. For Your Paternity has well shown many ways of interpreting Holy Scripture, but has not applied them to particular cases; without a doubt you would have encountered very great difficulties if you had wanted to interpret all those passages you yourself cited.

[172] Second, I say that, as you know, the Council[3] prohibits interpreting Scripture against the common consensus of the Holy Fathers; and if Your Paternity wants to read not only the Holy Fathers, but also the modern commentaries on Genesis, the Psalms, Ecclesiastes, and Joshua, you will find all agreeing in the literal interpretation that the sun is in heaven and turns around the earth with great speed, and that the earth is very far from heaven

---

1. Reprinted from Finocchiaro 1989, 67–69; cf. Galilei 1890–1909, 12: 171–72 (no. 1110).
2. I.e., in the third orbit around the sun.
3. The Council of Trent (1545–1563).

and sits motionless at the center of the world. Consider now, with your sense of prudence, whether the Church can tolerate giving Scripture a meaning contrary to the Holy Fathers and to all the Greek and Latin commentators. Nor can one answer that this is not a matter of faith, since if it is not a matter of faith "as regards the topic," it is a matter of faith "as regards the speaker";[4] and so it would be heretical to say that Abraham did not have two children and Jacob twelve, as well as to say that Christ was not born of a virgin, because both are said by the Holy Spirit through the mouth of the prophets and the apostles.

Third, I say that if there were a true demonstration that the sun is at the center of the world and the earth in the third heaven, and that the sun does not circle the earth but the earth circles the sun, then one would have to proceed with great care in explaining the Scriptures that appear contrary, and say rather that we do not understand them than that what is demonstrated is false. But I will not believe that there is such a demonstration, until it is shown me. Nor is it the same to demonstrate that by assuming the sun to be at the center and the earth in heaven one can save the appearances, and to demonstrate that in truth the sun is at the center and the earth in heaven; for I believe the first demonstration may be available, but I have very great doubts about the second, and in case of doubt one must not abandon the Holy Scripture as interpreted by the Holy Fathers.

I add that the one who wrote, "The sun also ariseth, and the sun goeth down, and hasteth to his place where he arose,"[5] was Solomon, who not only spoke inspired by God, but was a man above all others wise and learned in the human sciences and in the knowledge of created things; he received all this wisdom from God; therefore it is not likely that he was affirming something that was contrary to truth already demonstrated or capable of being demonstrated. Now, suppose you say that Solomon speaks in accordance with appearances, since it seems to us that the sun moves (while the earth does so), just as to someone who moves away from the seashore on a ship it looks like the shore is moving. I shall answer that when someone moves away from the shore, although it appears to him that the shore is moving away from him, nevertheless he knows that this is an error and corrects it, seeing clearly that the ship moves and not the shore; but in regard to the sun and the earth, no scientist has any need to correct the error, since he clearly experiences that the earth stands still and that the eye is not in error when it judges that the sun moves, as it also is not in error when it judges that the moon and the stars move. And this is enough for now.

---

4. Cf. Aquinas, *Summa theologica*, part ii of the second part, question 1, article 6 (1952, 84–85); Mayaud 2005, 3: 377–78, 6: 348–51.
5. Ecclesiastes 1:5 (King James Version).

With this I greet dearly Your Paternity, and I pray to God to grant you all your wishes.

§4. Galileo's Considerations on the Copernican Opinion (1615)[6]

[351] [§4.1] In order to remove (as much as the blessed God allows me) the occasion to deviate from the most correct judgment about the resolution of the pending controversy, I shall try to do away with two ideas. These are notions which I believe some are attempting to impress on the minds of those persons who are charged with the deliberations, and, if I am not mistaken, they are concepts far from the truth.

The first is that no one has any reason to fear that the outcome might be scandalous; for the earth's stability and sun's motion are so well demonstrated in philosophy that we can be sure and indubitably certain about them; on the other hand, the contrary position is such an immense paradox and obvious foolishness that no one can doubt in any way that it cannot be demonstrated now or ever, or indeed that it can never find a place in the mind of sensible persons. The other idea which they try to spread is the following: although that contrary assumption has been used by Copernicus and other astronomers, they did this in a suppositional manner and insofar as it can account more conveniently for the appearances of celestial motions and facilitate astronomical calculations and computations, and it is not the case that the same persons who assumed it believed it to be true de facto and in nature; so the conclusion is that one can safely proceed to condemning it. However, if I am not mistaken, these ideas are fallacious and far from the truth, as I can show with the following considerations. These will only be general and suitable to be understood without much effort and labor even by someone who is not well versed in the natural and astronomical sciences. For, if there were the opportunity to treat these [352] points with those who are very experienced in these studies, or at least who have the time to do the work required by the difficulty of the subject, then I should propose nothing but the reading of Copernicus's own book; from it and from the strength of his demonstrations one could clearly see how true or false are the two ideas we are discussing.

That it is not to be disparaged as ridiculous is, therefore, clearly shown by the quality of the men, both ancient and modern, who have held and do hold it. No one can regard it as ridiculous unless he considers ridiculous and foolish Pythagoras with all his school, Philolaus (teacher of Plato), Plato himself (as Aristotle testifies in his book *On the Heavens*), Heraclides of Pontus, Ecphantus, Aristarchus of Samos, Hicetas, and Seleucus the mathematician. Seneca

---

6. Reprinted from Finocchiaro 1989, 70–86; cf. Galilei 1890–1909, 5: 351–70.

himself not only does not ridicule it, but he makes fun of those who do, writing in his book *On Comets*: "It is also important to study these questions in order to learn whether the universe goes around the motionless earth, or the earth rotates but the universe does not. For some have said that we are naturally unaware of motion, that sunrise and sunset are not due to the motion of the heavens, but that it is we ourselves who rise and set. The matter deserves consideration, so that we may know the conditions of our existence, whether we stand still or move very fast, whether God drives everything around us or drives us."[7] Regarding the moderns, Nicolaus Copernicus first accepted it and amply confirmed it in his whole book. Then there were others: William Gilbert, a distinguished physician and philosopher, who treats it at length and confirms it in his book *On the Loadstone*;[8] Johannes Kepler, a living illustrious philosopher and mathematician in the service of the former and the current Emperor, follows the same opinion; Origanus (David Tost) at the beginning of his *Ephemerides*[9] supports the earth's motion with a very long discussion; and there is no lack of other authors who have published their reasons on the matter. Furthermore, though they have not published anything, I could name very many followers of this doctrine living in Rome, Florence, Venice, Padua, Naples, Pisa, Parma, and other places. This doctrine is not, therefore, ridiculous, having been accepted by great men; and, though their number is small compared to the followers of the common position, this is an indication of its being difficult to understand, rather than of its absurdity.

Moreover, that it is grounded on very powerful and effective [353] reasons may be shown from the fact that all its followers were previously of the contrary opinion, and indeed that for a long time they laughed at it and considered it foolish. Copernicus and I, and all others who are alive, are witnesses to this. Now, who will not believe that an opinion which is considered silly and indeed foolish, which has hardly one out of a thousand philosophers following it, and which is disapproved by the Prince of the prevailing philosophy, can become acceptable through anything but very firm demonstrations, very clear experiences, and very subtle observations? Certainly no one will be dissuaded of an opinion imbibed with mother's milk from his earliest training, accepted by almost the whole world and supported by the authority of very serious writers, unless the contrary reasons are more than effective. If we reflect carefully, we find that there is more value in the authority of a single person who follows the Copernican opinion than in that of one hundred others who hold

---

7. Cf. Seneca, *Quaestiones Naturales*, book vii, chapter 2.
8. William Gilbert, *De Magnete magneticisque corporibus et de magno magnete Tellure physiologia nova* (London, 1600).
9. *Origani novae coelestium motuum ephemerides* (Frankfurt, 1609); *ephemerides* (plural of *ephemeris*) are astronomical tables showing in a systematic way the positions of heavenly bodies at various times.

the contrary, since those who are persuaded of the truth of the Copernican system were in the beginning all very opposed. So I argue as follows.

Either those who are to be persuaded are capable of understanding the reasons of Copernicus and others who follow him, or they are not; moreover, either these reasons are true and demonstrative, or they are fallacious. If those who are to be persuaded are incapable, then they will never be persuaded by the true or by the false reasons; those who are capable of understanding the strength of the demonstrations will likewise never be persuaded if these demonstrations are fallacious; so neither those who do nor those who do not understand will be persuaded by fallacious reasons. Therefore, given that absolutely no one can be dissuaded from the first idea by fallacious reasons, it follows as a necessary consequence that, if anyone is persuaded of the contrary of what he previously believed, the reasons are persuasive and true. But as a matter of fact there are [354] many who are already persuaded by Copernican reasons. Therefore, it is true both that these reasons are effective, and that the opinion does not deserve the label of ridiculous but the label of worthy of being very carefully considered and pondered.

Furthermore, how futile it is to argue for the plausibility of this or that opinion simply from the large number of followers may be easily inferred from this: no one follows this opinion who did not previously believe the contrary; but instead you will not find even a single person who, after holding this opinion, will pass to the other one, regardless of any discussion he hears; consequently, one may judge, even if he does not understand the reasons for one side or for the other, that probably the demonstrations for the earth's motion are much stronger than those for the other side. But I shall say more, namely that if the probability of the two positions were something to be won by ballot, I would be willing to concede defeat when the opposite side had one more vote than I out of one hundred; not only that, but I would be willing to agree that every individual vote of the opponents was worth ten of mine, as long as the decision was made by persons who had perfectly heard, intimately penetrated, and subtly examined all the reasons and evidence of the two sides; indeed it is reasonable to expect that such would be those who cast the votes. Hence this opinion is not ridiculous and contemptible, but somewhat shaky is the position of whoever wanted to capitalize on the common opinion of the many who have not accurately studied these authors. What then should we say of the noises and the idle chatter of someone who has not understood even the first and simplest principles of these doctrines, and who is not qualified to understand them ever? What importance should we give him?

Consider now those who persist in wanting to say that as an astronomer Copernicus considered the earth's motion and the sun's stability only a hypothesis which is more adequate to save celestial appearances and to calculate the motions of planets, but that he did not believe it to be true in reality and in nature. With all due respect, these people show that they have been too prone to believe the word of someone who speaks more out of whim than out of experience with Copernicus's book or with understanding the nature of this business. For this reason they talk about it in a way that is not altogether right.

[355] First, limiting ourselves to general considerations, let us see his preface to Pope Paul III, to whom he dedicates the work. We shall find, to begin with, as if to comply with what they call the astronomer's task, that he had done and completed the work in accordance with the hypothesis of the prevailing philosophy and of Ptolemy himself, so that there was in it nothing lacking. But then, taking off the clothes of a pure astronomer and putting on those of a contemplator of nature, he undertook to examine whether this astronomical assumption already introduced, which was completely satisfactory regarding the calculations and the appearances of the motions of all planets, could also truly happen in the world and in nature. He found that in no way could such an arrangement of parts exist: although each by itself was well-proportioned, when they were put together the result was a very monstrous chimera. And so he began to investigate what the system of the world could really be in nature, no longer for the sole convenience of the pure astronomer, whose calculations he had complied with, but in order to come to an understanding of such a noble physical problem; he was confident that, if one had been able to account for mere appearances by means of hypotheses which are not true, this could be done much better by means of the true and physical constitution of the world. Having at his disposal a very large number of physically true and real observations of the motions of the stars (and without this knowledge it is wholly impossible to solve the problem), he worked tirelessly in search of such a constitution. Encouraged by the authority of so many great men, he examined the motion of the earth and the stability of the sun. Without their encouragement and authority, by himself either he would not have conceived the idea, or he would have considered it a very great absurdity and paradox, as he confesses to have considered it at first. But then, through long sensory observations, favorable results, and very firm demonstrations, he found it so consonant with the harmony of the world that he became completely certain of its truth. Hence this position is not introduced to satisfy the pure astronomer, but to satisfy the necessity of nature.

Furthermore, Copernicus knew and wrote in the same place that publishing this opinion would have made him look insane to the numberless followers of current philosophy, and especially to each and every [356] layman. Nevertheless, urged by the requests of the Cardinal of Capua[10] and the

---

10. Cardinal Nicolaus von Schoenberg (1472–1537), archbishop of Capua.

Bishop of Kulm,[11] he published it. Now, would he not have been really mad if, considering this opinion physically false, he had published that he believed it to be true, with the certain consequence that he would be regarded as a fool by the whole world? And why would he not have declared that he was using it only as an astronomer, but that he denied it as a philosopher, thus escaping the universal label of foolishness, to the advantage of his common sense?

Moreover, Copernicus states in great detail the grounds and reasons why the ancients believed the earth to be motionless, and then, examining the value of each in turn, he shows them to be ineffective. Now, who ever saw a sensible author engaged in confuting the demonstrations that confirm a proposition he considers true and real? And what kind of judgment would it be to criticize and to condemn a conclusion while in reality he wanted the reader to believe that he accepted it? This sort of incoherence cannot be attributed to such a man.

Furthermore, note carefully that, since we are dealing with the motion or stability of the earth or of the sun, we are in a dilemma of contradictory propositions (one of which has to be true), and we cannot in any way resort to saying that perhaps it is neither this way nor that way. Now, if the earth's stability and sun's motion are de facto physically true and the contrary position is absurd, how can one reasonably say that the false view agrees better than the true one with the phenomena clearly visible and sensed in the movements and arrangement of the stars? Who does not know that there is a most agreeable harmony among all truths of nature, and a most sharp dissonance between false positions and true effects? Will it happen, then, that the earth's motion and sun's stability agree in every way with the arrangement of all other bodies in the universe and with all the phenomena, a thousand of them, which we and our predecessors have observed in great detail, and that this position is false? And can the earth's stability and sun's motion be considered true and not agree in any way with the other truths? If one could say that neither this nor that position is true, it might happen that one would be more convenient than the other in accounting for the appearances. But, given two [357] positions, one of which must be true and the other false, to say that the false one agrees better with the effects of nature is really something that surpasses my imagination. I add: if Copernicus confesses to having fully satisfied astronomers by means of the hypothesis commonly accepted as true, how can one say that by means of the false and foolish one he could or would want to satisfy again the same astronomers?

However, I now go on to consider the nature of the business from an internal viewpoint, and to show with how much care one must discuss it.

---

11. Tiedemann Giese (1480–1550), Polish friend of Copernicus.

Astronomers have so far made two sorts of suppositions: some are primary and pertain to the absolute truth of nature; others are secondary and are imagined in order to account for the appearances of stellar motions, which appearances seem not to agree with the primary and true assumptions. For example, before trying to account for the appearances, acting not as a pure astronomer but as a pure philosopher, Ptolemy supposes, indeed he takes from philosophers, that celestial movements are all circular and regular, namely uniform; that heaven has a spherical shape; that the earth is at the center of the celestial sphere, is spherical, motionless, etc. Turning then to the inequalities we see in planetary movements and distances, which seem to clash with the primary physical suppositions already established, he goes on to another sort of supposition; these aim to identify the reasons why, without changing the primary ones, there is such a clear and sensible inequality in the movements of planets and in their approaching and their moving away from the earth. To do this he introduces some motions that are still circular, but around centers other than the earth's, tracing eccentric and epicyclic circles. This secondary supposition is the one of which it could be said that the astronomer supposes it to facilitate his computations, without committing himself to maintaining that it is true in reality and in nature.

Let us now see in what kind of hypothesis Copernicus places the earth's motion and sun's stability. There is no doubt whatever, if we reflect carefully, that he places it among the primary and necessary suppositions about nature. For, as I have already stated, it seems that he had already given satisfaction to astronomers by the other road, and that he takes this one only to try to solve the greatest problem [358] of nature. In fact, to say that he makes this supposition to facilitate astronomical calculations is so false that instead we can see him, when he comes to these calculations, leaving this supposition and returning to the old one, the latter being more readily and easily understood and still very quick even in computations. This may be seen as follows. Intrinsically, particular calculations can be made by taking one position as well as the other, that is, by making the earth or the heavens rotate; nevertheless, many geometers and astronomers in many books have already demonstrated the properties of orthogonal and oblique displacements of parts of the zodiac in relation to the equator, the declinations of the parts of the ecliptic, the variety of angles between it and both meridians and oblique horizons, and a thousand other specific details necessary to complete astronomical science. This ensures that, when he comes to examining these details of the primary motions, Copernicus himself examines them in the old manner, namely as occurring along circles traced in the heavens and around the motionless earth, even though stillness and stability should belong to the highest heaven, called the Prime Mobile, and motion to the earth. Thus in the introduction to Book Two he concludes: "Let nobody be surprised if I still refer simply to the rising and setting of the sun and stars, and similar phenomena. On the contrary, it will be recognized that I use the customary terminology, which can be accepted by everybody. Yet I always bear in mind that 'for us who are borne by the earth, the sun and the moon pass by, and the stars return on their rounds, and again they drop out of sight'."[12]

We should therefore understand clearly that Copernicus takes the earth's motion and sun's stability for no other reason and in no other way than to establish it, in the manner of the natural philosopher, as a hypothesis of the primary sort; on the contrary, when he comes to astronomical computations, he goes back to the old hypothesis, which takes the circles of the basic motions with their details to be located in the highest heaven around the motionless earth, being easier for everyone to understand on account of ingrained habit. But what am I saying? Such is the strength of truth and the weakness of false-hood, that those who speak this way reveal themselves not completely capable of understanding these subjects and not well versed in them; this happens when they let themselves be persuaded that the secondary kind of hypothesis is con-sidered chimerical and fictional by Ptolemy and by other serious astronomers, [359] and that they really regard them as physically false and introduced only for the sake of astronomical computations. The only support they give for this very fanciful opinion is a passage in Ptolemy where, unable to observe more than one simple anomaly in the sun, he wrote that to account for it one could take the hypothesis of a simple eccentric as well as that of an epicycle on a con-centric, and he added he preferred the first for being simpler than the second; from these words some very superficially argue that Ptolemy did not consider necessary, but rather wholly fictional, both this and that supposition, since he said they are both equally convenient, while one and only one can be attrib-uted to the sun's behavior. But what kind of superficiality is this? Who can do both of the following? First, to suppose as true the primary suppositions that planetary motions are circular and regular, and to admit (as the senses them-selves necessarily force us) that in running through the zodiac all planets are now slow and now fast, indeed that most of them can be not only slow but also stationary and retrograde,[13] and that we see them now very large and very near the earth and now very small and very far; and then, having understood these former points, to deny that eccentrics and epicycles can really exist in nature? This is wholly excusable for men who are not specialists in these sciences, but for others who would claim to be experts in them it would be an indication

---

12. Here quoted from Copernicus 1992, 51.
13. Retrograde motion is westward motion against the background of the fixed stars, which a planet appears to have periodically for brief periods, thus reversing its usually eastward motion (called direct motion); in the geostatic system, retrograde motion was explained by means of epicycles; in the Copernican system, it is explained in terms of the relative motion between the earth and the planet in question.

that they do not even understand the meaning of the terms *eccentric* and *epicycle*. One might just as well first admit that there are three letters, the first of which is *G*, the second *O*, and the third *D*, and then at the end deny that their combination yields *GOD* and claim that the result is *SHADOW*.

But if rational arguments were not sufficient to make one understand the necessity of having to place eccentrics and epicycles really in nature, at least the senses themselves would have to persuade him: for we see the four Medicean planets trace four small circles around Jupiter which are very far from enclosing the earth, in short, four epicycles; Venus, which is seen now full of light and now very thinly crescent, provides conclusive evidence that its revolution is around the sun and not around the earth, and consequently that its orbit is an epicycle; and the same may be argued for the case of Mercury. Moreover, the three outer planets are [360] very near the earth when they are in opposition to the sun, and very far when in conjunction; for example, Mars at its closest appears to the senses more than fifty times larger than at its farthest, so that some have occasionally feared that it had gotten lost or had vanished, being really invisible because of its great distance; now, what else can one conclude but that their revolution is made in eccentric circles, or in epicycles, or in a combination of the two, if we take the second anomaly into consideration? So, to deny eccentrics and epicycles in the motions of planets is like denying the light of the sun, or else it is to contradict oneself.

Let us apply what I am saying more directly to our purpose: some say that modern astronomers introduce the earth's motion and sun's stability suppositionally in order to save the appearances and to facilitate calculations, just as epicycles and eccentrics are assumed in the same manner, though the same astronomers consider them physically chimerical and repugnant; I answer that I shall gladly agree with all this talk, as long as they limit themselves to staying within their own conceptions, namely that the earth's motion and sun's stability is as false or true in nature as epicycles and eccentrics. Let them, then, make every effort to do away with the true and real existence of these circles, for if they succeed in demonstrating their nonexistence in nature, I shall immediately surrender and admit the earth's motion to be a great absurdity. But if, on the contrary, they are forced to accept them, let them also accept the earth's motion, and let them admit to have been convinced by their own contradictions.

I could present many other things for this same purpose. However, since I think that whoever is not persuaded by what I have said would not be persuaded by many more reasons either, I want these to suffice. I shall only add something about what could have been the motive some have concluded with any plausibility that Copernicus himself did not really believe his own hypothesis.

There is on the reverse side of the title page of Copernicus's book a certain preface to the reader, which is not by the author since it mentions him in
the third person and is without signature.[14] It clearly states that no one should
believe in the least that Copernicus regarded his position as true, but only that he
feigned [361] and introduced it for the calculation of celestial motions; it ends its
discussion by concluding that to hold it as true and real would be foolish. This
conclusion is so explicit that whoever reads no further, and believes it to have
been placed at least with the author's consent, deserves to be somewhat excused
for his error. But what weight to give to the opinion of those who would judge
a book without reading anything but a brief preface by the printer or publisher,
I let each one decide for himself. I say that this preface can only have originated
from the publisher to facilitate the sale of a book which common people would
have regarded as a fanciful chimera if a similar preface had not been added; for
most of the time buyers are in the habit of reading such prefaces before buy-
ing the work. Not only was this preface not written by the author, but it was
included without his consent, and also without his knowledge; this is shown by
the errors it contains, which the author would have never committed.

This preface says no one can consider it verisimilar, unless he is completely ignorant of geometry and optics, that Venus has such a large epicycle
enabling it now to precede and now to follow the sun by forty degrees or
more; for it would have to happen that when it is highest its diameter should
appear only one-fourth of what it appears when it is lowest, and that in the
latter location its body should be seen as sixteen times bigger than in the
former; but these things, he says, are repugnant to the observations made
throughout the centuries. In these assertions we see, first, that the writer
does not know that Venus departs on one side and on the other of the sun
by about forty-eight degrees, and not forty as he says. Moreover, he asserts
that its diameter should appear four times, and its body sixteen times, larger
in one position than in the other. Here, first, due to a geometrical oversight he does not understand that when a globe has a diameter four times
larger than another, its body is sixty-four times bigger, and not sixteen, as
he stated. Hence, if he considered such an epicycle absurd and wanted to
declare it to be physically impossible, if he had understood this subject, he
could have made the absurdity much greater; for, according to the position he wants to refute (well known to astronomers), Venus digresses from
the sun almost forty-eight degrees, and when farthest from the earth its
distance [362] must be more than six times greater than when closest, and
consequently its apparent diameter in the latter position is more than six

---

14. This preface was in fact written by Andreas Osiander (1498–1552), a Lutheran
theologian who supervised the last phase of the printing of Copernicus's book at
Nuremberg; the action was soon discovered by Copernicus's friends and followers,
causing a controversy, but it did not become generally known for some time.

times larger than in the former (not four times), and its body more than two hundred and sixteen times greater (and not just sixteen). These errors are so gross that it is impossible to believe they were committed by Copernicus, or by anyone else but the most unqualified persons. Moreover, why label such a large epicycle most absurd, so that because of such an absurdity we would conclude that Copernicus did not regard his assumptions as true, and that neither should others so regard them? He should have remembered that in chapter 10 of the first book Copernicus is speaking *ad hominem* and is attacking other astronomers who allege that it is a great absurdity to give Venus such an epicycle, which is so large as to exceed the whole lunar orbit by more than two hundred times, and which does not contain anything inside; he then removes the absurdity when he shows that inside Venus's orbit is contained the orbit of Mercury and, placed at the center, the body of the sun itself. What frivolity is this, then, to want to show a position mistaken and false on account of a difficulty which that position not only does not introduce in nature, but completely removes? Similarly it removes the immense epicycles which out of necessity other astronomers assumed in the other system. This only touches the writer of Copernicus's preface; so we may argue that, if he had included something else professionally relevant, he would have committed other errors.

But finally, to remove any shadow of a doubt, if the failure to observe such great variations in the apparent sizes of the body of Venus should cast doubt on its circular revolution around the sun (in conformity with the Copernican system),[15] then let us make careful observations with a suitable instrument, namely with a good telescope, and we shall find all effects and experiences exactly agreeing; that is, we shall see Venus crescent when it is nearest to the earth, and with a diameter six times larger than when it is at its maximum distance, namely above the sun, where it is seen round and very small. I have discussed elsewhere the reasons for not detecting these variations with our simple eyesight, but just as from this failure we could reasonably deny that supposition, so now, from seeing the very exact correspondence in this and every other detail, we should abandon any doubt and consider the supposition true and real. As for the rest of this admirable [363] system, whoever desires to ascertain the opinion of Copernicus himself should not read the fanciful preface of the printer, but the whole work of the author himself; without a doubt he will grasp first-hand that Copernicus held as very true the stability of the sun and the motion of the earth.

[364] [§4.2] The motion of the earth and stability of the sun could never be against Faith or Holy Scripture, if it were correctly proved to be physically true by philosophers, astronomers, and mathematicians, with the help of sense

---

15. Here, my earlier translation (Finocchiaro 1989, 80) of this last clause has been improved, following a suggestion by Mario Biagioli (private correspondence).

experiences, accurate observations, and necessary demonstrations. However, in this case, if some passages of Scripture were to sound contrary, we would have to say that this is due to the weakness of our mind, which is unable to grasp the true meaning of Scripture in this particular case. This is the common doctrine, and it is entirely right, since one truth cannot contradict another truth. On the other hand, whoever wants to condemn it judicially must first demonstrate it to be physically false by collecting the reasons against it.

Now, one wants to know where to begin in order to ascertain its falsity, that is, whether from the authority of Scripture or from the refutation of the demonstrations and observations of philosophers and astronomers. I answer that one must start from the place which is safest and least likely to bring about a scandal; this means beginning with physical and mathematical arguments. For if the reasons proving the earth's motion are found fallacious, and the contrary ones conclusive, then we have already become certain of the falsity of this proposition and of the truth of the opposite, which we now say corresponds to the meaning of Scripture; so one would be free to condemn the false proposition and there would be no danger. But if those reasons are found true and necessary, this will not bring any harm to the authority of Scripture; instead we shall have been cautioned that due to our ignorance we had not grasped the true sense of Scripture, and that we can learn this meaning with the help of the newly acquired physical truth. Therefore, beginning with the arguments is safe in any case. On the other hand, if we were to fix only on what seemed to us the true and certain meaning of Scripture, and we were to go on to condemn such a proposition without examining the strength of the arguments, what a scandal would follow if sensible experiences and reasons were to show the opposite? And who would have brought confusion to [365] the Holy Church? Those who had suggested the greatest consideration of the arguments, or those who had disparaged them? One can see, then, which road is safer.

Moreover, we admit that a physical proposition which has been proved true by physical and mathematical demonstrations can never contradict Scripture, but that in such a case it is the weakness of our mind which prevents us from grasping its true meaning. On the other hand, whoever wants to use the authority of the same passages of Scripture to confute and prove false the same proposition would commit the error called "begging the question."[16] For, the true meaning of Scripture being in doubt in the light of the arguments, one cannot take it as clear and certain in order to refute the same proposition; instead one must cripple the arguments and find the fallacies with the help of

---

16. Begging the question is the fallacy of assuming, in the course of a dispute, the truth of what is being questioned; thus, for example, if part of the dispute is about what is the correct meaning of a particular scriptural passage, then to argue against the earth's motion on the basis of a given meaning of that passage would be to beg the question.

other reasons and experiences and more certain observations. When the factual and physical truth has been found in this manner, then, and not before, can one be assured of the true meaning of Scripture and safely use it. Thus the safe road is to begin with the arguments, confirming the true and refuting the fallacious ones.

If the earth de facto moves, we cannot change nature and arrange for it not to move. But we can rather easily remove the opposition of Scripture with the mere admission that we do not grasp its true meaning. Therefore, the way to be sure not to err is to begin with astronomical and physical investigations, and not with scriptural ones.

I am always told that, in interpreting the passages of Scripture relevant to this point, all Fathers agree to the meaning which is simplest and corresponds to the literal meaning; hence, presumably, it is improper to give them another meaning or to change the common interpretation, because this would amount to accusing the Fathers of carelessness or negligence. I answer by admitting that the Fathers indeed deserve reasonable and proper respect, but I add that we have an excuse for them very readily: it is that on this subject they never interpreted Scripture differently from the literal meaning, because at their time the opinion of the earth's motion was totally buried, and no one even talked about it, let alone wrote about it or maintained it. But there is no trace of negligence by the Fathers for not thinking about what was completely hidden. That they did not think about it is [366] clear from the fact that in their writings one cannot find even a word about this opinion. And if anyone were to say that they considered it, this would make its condemnation more dangerous; for after considering it, not only did they not condemn it, but they did not express any doubt about it.

Thus the defense of the Fathers is readily available and very easy. On the contrary, it would be very difficult or impossible to excuse or exonerate from a similar charge of carelessness the Popes, Councils, and Congregations of the Index of the last eighty years, if this doctrine were erroneous and deserving of condemnation; for they have let this opinion circulate[17] in a book which was first written on orders from a Pope, and then printed on orders from a cardinal and a bishop, dedicated to another Pope, and, most important, received by the Holy Church, so that one cannot say that it had remained unknown. If, then, the inappropriateness of charging our highest authorities with negligence is to be taken into account, as it should, let us make sure that in trying to escape one absurdity we do not fall into a greater one.

---

17. This statement is literally correct, but Copernicus's book came close to being prohibited immediately after its publication; this did not happen because of the death of the officials involved. See Beltrán Marí 2006, 124–30; Westman 2011, 194–97.

But assume now that someone regards it as inappropriate to abandon the unanimous interpretation of the Fathers, even in the case of physical propositions not discussed by them and whose opposite they did not even consider; I then ask what one should do if necessary demonstrations showed the facts of nature to be the opposite. Which of the two decrees should be changed? The one which stipulates that no proposition can be both true and erroneous, or the other one which obliges us to regard as articles of faith physical propositions supported by the unanimous interpretation of the Fathers? It seems to me, if I am not mistaken, that it would be safer to modify this second decree than to be forced to hold as an article of faith a physical proposition which had been demonstrated with conclusive reasons to be factually false in nature. It also seems to me that one could say that the unanimous interpretation of the Fathers should have absolute authority in the case of propositions which they aired, and for which no contrary demonstrations exist and it is certain that none could ever exist. I do not bring in the fact that it is very clear that the Council[18] requires only that one agree with the unanimous interpretation of the Fathers "in matters of faith and morals, etc."

[367] [§4.3] 1. Copernicus uses eccentrics and epicycles, but these were not the reason for rejecting the Ptolemaic system, since they undoubtedly exist in the heavens; it was other difficulties.

2. In regard to philosophers, if they were true philosophers, namely lovers of truth, they should not get irritated, but, learning that they were wrong, they should thank whoever shows them the truth; and if their opinion were to stand up, they would have reason to take pride in it, rather than being irritated. Theologians should not get irritated because, if this opinion were found false then they could freely prohibit it, and if it were discovered true then they should rejoice that others have found the way to understand the true meaning of Scripture and have restrained them from perpetrating a serious scandal by condemning a true proposition.

In regard to falsifying Scripture, this is not and will never be the intention of Catholic astronomers such as ourselves; rather our view is that Scripture corresponds very well to truths demonstrated about nature. Moreover, certain theologians who are not astronomers should be careful about falsifying Scripture by wanting to interpret it as opposed to propositions which may be true and demonstrable.

3. It might happen that we could have difficulties in interpreting Scripture, but this would occur because of our ignorance, and not because there really are or can be insuperable difficulties in reconciling them with demonstrated truths.

---

18. The Council of Trent (1545–1563).

4. The Council speaks "about matters of faith and morals, etc." So there is an answer to saying that such a proposition is "an article of faith by reason of the speaker," though not "by reason of the topic," and that therefore it is among those covered by the Council. The answer is that everything in Scripture is "an article of faith by reason of the speaker," so that in this regard it should be included in the rule of the Council; but this clearly has not been done because in that case it would have said that "the interpretation of the Fathers is to be followed for every word of Scripture, etc.," and not "for matters of faith and morals"; having thus said "for matters of faith," we see that its intention was to mean "for matters of faith by reason of the topic."

Then consider that [368] it is much more a matter of faith to hold that Abraham had some children and that Tobias had a dog, because Scripture says it, than it would be to hold that the earth moves, even if this were found in the same Scripture, and further that to deny the former is a heresy, but not to deny the latter. It seems to me that this depends on the following reason. There have always been in the world men who had two, four, six children, etc., or none, and similarly people who have dogs and who do not, so that it is equally credible that some have children or dogs and others do not; hence there appears to be no reason why in such propositions the Holy Spirit should speak differently from the truth, the negative and the affirmative sides being equally credible to all men. But it is not so with the motion of the earth and the stability of the sun; for these propositions are very far removed from the understanding of the masses, and on these matters not relevant to their eternal life the Holy Spirit chose to conform its pronouncements with their abilities, even when facts are otherwise from the point of view of the thing in itself.

5. In regard to placing the sun in heaven and the earth outside it, as Scripture seems to affirm, etc., this truly seems to me to be a simple perception of ours and a manner of speaking only for our convenience. For, in reality all that is surrounded by heaven is in heaven, just as all that is surrounded by the city walls is in the city; indeed, if one were to express a preference, what is in the middle is more in heaven and in the city, being, as it were, at the heart of the city and of heaven. That difference exists because one takes the elemental region surrounding the earth as being very different from the celestial region. But such a difference will always exist regardless of where these elements are placed; and it will always be true that from the viewpoint of our convenience the earth is below us and heaven above, since all the inhabitants of the earth have heaven above our heads, which is our upwards, and the center of the earth under our feet, which is our downwards; so, in relation to us the center of the earth and the surface of heaven are the farthest places, that is, the endpoints of our up and down, which are diametrically opposite points.

6. Not to believe that there is a demonstration of the earth's mobility until it is shown is very prudent, nor do we ask that anyone believe such a

thing without a demonstration. On the contrary, we only seek that, for the advantage of the Holy Church, one examine with [369] the utmost severity what the followers of this doctrine know and can advance, and that nothing be granted them unless the strength of their arguments greatly exceeds that of the reasons for the opposite side. Now, if they are not more than ninety percent right, they may be dismissed; but if all that is produced by philosophers and astronomers on the opposite side is shown to be mostly false and wholly inconsequential, then the other side should not be disparaged, nor deemed paradoxical, so as to think that it could never be clearly proved. It is proper to make such a generous offer since it is clear that those who hold the false side cannot have in their favor any valid reason or experiment, whereas it is necessary that all things agree and correspond with the true side.

7. It is true that it is not the same to show that one can save the appearances with the earth's motion and the sun's stability, and to demonstrate that these hypotheses are really true in nature. But it is equally true, or even more so, that one cannot account for such appearances with the other commonly accepted system. The latter is undoubtedly false, while it is clear that the former, which can account for them, may be true. Nor can or should one seek any greater truth in a position than that it corresponds with all particular appearances.

8. One is not asking that in case of doubt the interpretation of the Fathers should be abandoned, but only that an attempt be made to gain certainty regarding what is in doubt, and that therefore no one disparage what attracts and has attracted very great philosophers and astronomers. Then, after all necessary care has been taken, the decision may be made.

9. We believe that Solomon, Moses, and all other sacred writers knew perfectly the constitution of the world, as they also knew that God has no hands, no feet, and no experience of anger, forgetfulness, or regret; nor will we ever doubt this. But we say what the Holy Fathers and in particular Saint Augustine say about these matters, namely that the Holy Spirit inspired them to write what they wrote for various reasons, etc.

10. The error of the apparent movement of the shore and stability of the ship is known by us after having many times observed the motion of boats from the shore, and many other times observed the shore from a boat; and so, if we could now stay on earth and now go to the sun [370] or other star, perhaps we would acquire sensible and certain knowledge of which one of them moves. To be sure, if we looked only at these two bodies, it would always seem to us that the one we were on was standing still, just as looking only at the water and the boat always gives the appearance that the water is flowing and the boat is standing still. Moreover, the two situations are very different: there is great disparity between a small boat, separable from its environment, and the immense shore, known by us through thousands of experiences to be

motionless, that is, motionless in relation to the water and the boat; but the other comparison is between two bodies both of which are substantial and equally inclined toward motion and toward rest. Thus it would be more relevant to compare between themselves two boats, in which case it is absolutely certain that the one we were on would always appear to us as motionless, as long as we could not consider any other relationship but that which holds between these two ships.

There is, therefore, a very great need to correct the error about observing whether the earth or else the sun moves, for it is clear that to someone on the moon or any other planet it would always appear that it was standing still and the other stars were moving. But these and many other more plausible reasons of the followers of the common opinion are the ones that must be untied very openly, before one can pretend even to be heard, let alone approved; unfortunately we have not done a very detailed examination of what is produced against us. Moreover, neither Copernicus nor his followers will ever use this phenomenon of the shore and the boat to prove that the earth is in motion and the sun at rest. They only adduce it as an example that serves to show, not the truth of their position, but the absence of contradiction between the appearance of a stable earth and moving sun to our simple sense experience, and the reality of the contrary. For, if this were one of Copernicus's demonstrations, or if his others did not argue more effectively, I really think that no one would agree with him.

CHAPTER 3

Earlier Proceedings: Prohibition of Copernicanism

§5. Lorini's Complaint (7 February 1615)[1]

[297] Most Illustrious and Most Reverend Lord:[2]

Besides the common duty of every good Christian, there is a limitless obligation that binds all Dominican friars, since they were designated by the Holy Father the black and white hounds of the Holy Office. This applies in particular to all theologians and preachers, and hence to me, lowest of all and most devoted to Your Most Illustrious Lordship.

I have come across a letter[3] that is passing through everybody's hands here, originating among those known as "Galileists," who, following the views of Copernicus, affirm that the earth moves and the heavens stand still. In the judgment of all our Fathers at this very religious convent of Saint Mark, it contains many propositions which to us seem either suspect or rash: for example, that certain ways of speaking in the Holy Scripture are inappropriate; that in disputes about natural effects the same Scripture holds the last place; that its expositors are often wrong in their interpretations; that the same Scripture must not meddle with anything else but articles concerning faith; and that, in questions about natural phenomena, philosophical or astronomical argument has more force than the sacred and the divine one. Your Most Illustrious Lordship can see these propositions underlined by me in the above-mentioned letter, of which I send you a faithful copy.[4] Finally, it claims that when Joshua ordered the sun to stop one must understand that the order was given to the Prime Mobile and not to the sun itself.

Besides this letter passing through everybody's hands, without being stopped by any of the authorities, it seems to me that some want to expound

---

1. Reprinted from Finocchiaro 1989, 134–35; cf. Galilei 1890–1909, 19: 297–98.
2. Paolo Sfondrati.
3. Galileo's letter to Castelli of 21 December 1613 (§1 above).
4. The copy of Galileo's letter to Castelli enclosed by Lorini differs somewhat from the one regarded as the most genuine copy by Antonio Favaro, the chief editor of the critical edition of Galileo's complete works (Galilei 1890–1909); the Favaro copy is the one translated above. For the precise differences, see Finocchiaro 1989, 331 n. 16; on the question of authenticity, see Pesce 1992 and Finocchiaro (1989, 55).

Holy Scripture in their own way and against the common exposition of the Holy Fathers and to defend [298] an opinion apparently wholly contrary to Holy Scripture. Moreover, I hear that they speak disrespectfully of the ancient Holy Fathers and Saint Thomas; that they trample underfoot all of Aristotle's philosophy, which is so useful to scholastic theology; and that to appear clever they utter and spread a thousand impertinences around our whole city, kept so Catholic by its own good nature and by the vigilance of our Most Serene Princes.

For these reasons I resolved, as I said, to send it to Your Most Illustrious Lordship, who is filled with the most holy zeal and who, for the position that you occupy, is responsible, together with your most illustrious colleagues, for keeping your eyes open in such matters; thus if it seems to you that there is any need for correction, you may find those remedies that you judge necessary, in order that a small error at the beginning does not become great at the end. Though perhaps I could have sent you a copy of some notes on the said letter made at this convent, nevertheless, out of modesty I refrained since I was writing to you who know so much and to Rome where, as Saint Bernard said, the holy faith has lynx eyes.

I declare that I regard all those who are called Galileists as men of goodwill and good Christians, but a little conceited and fixed in their opinions; similarly, I state that in taking this action I am moved by nothing but zeal. I also beg Your Most Illustrious Lordship that this letter of mine (I am not referring to the other letter mentioned above) be kept secret by you, as I am sure you will, and that it be regarded not as a judicial deposition but only as a friendly notice between you and me, like between a servant and a special patron. And I also inform you that the occasion of my writing was one or two public sermons given in our church of Santa Maria Novella by Father Tommaso Caccini, commenting on the book of Joshua and chapter 10 of the said book. So I close by asking for your holy blessing, kissing your garment, and asking for a particle of your holy prayers.

§6. Caccini's Deposition (20 March 1615)[5]

[307] There appeared personally and of his own accord at Rome in the great hall of examinations in the palace of the Holy Office, in the presence of the Reverend Father Michelangelo Segizzi, O.P., Master of Sacred Theology and Commissary General of the Holy Roman and Universal Inquisition, etc., the Reverend Father Tommaso Caccini, son of the late Giovanni Caccini, Florentine, a professed priest of the Order of Preachers, Master and Bachelor

---

5. Reprinted from Finocchiaro 1989, 136–41; cf. Galilei 1890–1909, 19: 307–11.

from the convent of Santa Maria sopra Minerva in Rome, about thirty-nine years of age. Having been administered the oath to tell the truth, he declared as follows:

I had spoken with the Most Illustrious Lord Cardinal Aracoeli about some things taking place in Florence, and yesterday he sent for me and told me that I should come here and tell everything to you. Since I was told that a legal deposition is needed, I am here for this purpose. I say then that on the fourth Sunday of Advent of this past year I was preaching at the church of Santa Maria Novella in Florence, where I had been assigned by superiors this year as a reader of Holy Scripture, and I continued with the story of Joshua begun earlier. Precisely on this Sunday, I happened to read the passage of the tenth chapter of that book where the sacred writer relates the great miracle which God made in answer to Joshua's prayers by stopping the sun, namely "Sun, stand thou still upon Gibeon,"[6] etc. After interpreting this passage first in a literal sense and then in accordance with its spiritual intention for the salvation of souls, I took the opportunity to criticize, with that modesty which befits the office I held, a certain view once proposed by Nicolaus Copernicus and nowadays held and taught by Mr. Galileo Galilei, mathematician, according to public opinion very widespread in the city of Florence. This is the view that the sun, being [308] for him the center of the world, is immovable as regards progressive local motion, that is, motion from one place to another. I said that such a view is regarded as discordant with Catholic faith by very serious writers, since it contradicts many passages of the divine Scripture whose literal sense, as given unanimously by the Holy Fathers, sounds and means the opposite; for example, the passage of the 18th Psalm,[7] of the first chapter of Ecclesiastes, of Isaiah 38, besides the Joshua passage cited. And in order to impress upon the audience that such a teaching of mine did not originate from my whim, I read them Nicolaus Serarius's doctrine (fourteenth question on chapter 10 of Joshua): after saying that such a position of Copernicus is contrary to the common account of almost all philosophers, all scholastic theologians, and all the Holy Fathers, he added that he could not see how such an opinion is not almost heretical, due to the above-mentioned passages of Scripture. After this discussion I cautioned them that no one was allowed to interpret divine Scripture in a way contrary to the sense on which all the Holy Fathers agree, since this was prohibited both by the Lateran Council under Leo X and by the Council of Trent.

Although this charitable warning of mine greatly pleased many educated and devout gentlemen, it displeased certain disciples of the above-mentioned

---

6. Joshua 10:12.
7. Psalms 18:6–7 (Douay Version), corresponding to Psalms 19:6–7 (King James Version).

Galilei beyond measure; thus, some of them approached the preacher at the cathedral so that he would preach on this topic against the doctrine I expounded. Having heard so many rumors, out of zeal for the truth, I reported to the very reverend Father Inquisitor of Florence what my conscience had led me to discuss concerning the Joshua passage; I also suggested to him that it would be good to restrain certain petulant minds, disciples of the said Galilei, of whom the reverend Father Fra Ferdinando Ximenes, regent of Santa Maria Novella, had told me that from some of them he had heard these three propositions: "God is not otherwise a substance, but an accident"; "God is sensuous because there are in him divine senses"; and, "in truth the miracles said to have been made by the saints are not real miracles."

After these events, Father Master Fra Niccolò Lorini showed me a copy of a letter written by the above-mentioned Mr. Galileo Galilei to Father Benedetto Castelli, Benedictine monk and professor of mathematics at Pisa, in which it seemed to me are contained questionable doctrines in the domain of theology. Since a copy of it was sent to the Lord Cardinal of Santa Cecilia,[8] I have nothing else to add to that.

Thus, I declare to this Holy Office that it is a widespread opinion that the above-mentioned Galilei holds these two propositions: the earth moves as a whole as well as with diurnal motion; the sun is motionless. These are propositions which, according to my [309] conscience and understanding, are repugnant to the divine Scriptures expounded by the Holy Fathers and consequently to the Faith, which teaches that we must believe as true what is contained in Scripture. And for now I have nothing else to say.

He was asked: How he knows that Galileo teaches and holds the sun to be motionless and the earth to move, and whether he learned this expressly from others.

He answered: Aside from public notoriety, as I said before, I also heard from Mons. Filippo de' Bardi, Bishop of Cortona, at the time I stayed there and then in Florence, that Galilei holds the above-mentioned propositions as true; he added that this seemed to him very strange, as not agreeing with Scripture. I also heard it from a certain Florentine gentleman of the Attavanti family, a follower of the same Galilei, who said to me that Galilei interpreted Scripture in such a way as not to conflict with his opinion. I do not recall this gentleman's name, nor do I know where his house is in Florence; I am sure that he often comes to service at Santa Maria Novella in Florence, that he wears priest's clothes, and that he is twenty-eight or thirty years of age perhaps, of olive complexion, chestnut beard, average height, and sharply delineated face. He told it to me this past summer, about the month of August, in Father Ferdinando Ximenes' room, the occasion being that Father Ximenes

---

8. Paolo Sfondrati.

was telling me that I should not take too long discussing the miracle of the stopping of the sun when he (Ximenes) was around. I have also read this doctrine in a book printed in Rome, dealing with sunspots, published under the name of the said Galileo, and lent to me by the said Father Ximenes.

Q:[9] Who the preacher at the cathedral is, to whom Galileo's disciples went in order to have a public sermon against the doctrine taught equally publicly by the plaintiff himself, and who those disciples are who made such a request to the said preacher.

A: The preacher at the Florence cathedral whom Galileo's disciples approached about preaching against the doctrine I taught is a Jesuit Father from Naples, whose name I do not know. Nor have I learned these things from the said preacher, since I did not even speak with him. Rather they have been told me by Father Emanuele Ximenes, a Jesuit, whom the said preacher had asked for advice, and who dissuaded him. Nor do I know who were the disciples of Galilei who contacted the preacher about the above-mentioned matters.

Q: Whether he has ever talked to the said Galileo.

A: I do not even know what he looks like.

Q: What the reputation of the said Galileo is in the city of Florence regarding matters of faith.

A: By many he is regarded as a good Catholic. By others he is regarded with suspicion in matters of faith because they say he is very close to Fra Paolo,[10] of the Servite order, so [310] famous in Venice for his impieties; and they say that letters are exchanged between them even now.

Q: Whether he remembers from which person or persons he learned about these matters.

A: I heard these things from Father Master Niccolò Lorini and from another Mr. Ximenes,[11] Prior of the Knights of Santo Stefano. They told me the above-mentioned things. That is, Father Niccolò Lorini has repeated to me several times and even written to me here in Rome that between Galileo and Master Paolo there is an exchange of letters and great friendship, and that the latter is a suspect in matters of faith. And Prior Ximenes did not tell me anything different about the closeness between Master Paolo and Galileo, but only that Galilei is a suspect and that, while being in Rome once, he learned how the Holy Office was trying to seize him, on account of which he ran away. This was told me in the room of the above-mentioned Father

---

9. Note that, here and in subsequent depositions, the letter Q is meant as an abbreviation for the sentence "He was asked," which yields, together with the expression that follows, an *indirect* rather than a direct question.

10. Paolo Sarpi.

11. Sebastiano Ximenes, not to be confused with either one of the two other persons with the same surname mentioned earlier, Ferdinando Ximenes and Emanuele Ximenes.

Ferdinando, his cousin, though I do not remember exactly if the said Father was present there.

Q: Whether he learned from the above-mentioned Father Lorini and the Knight Ximenes why they regarded the said Galileo to be suspect in matters of faith.

A: They did not say anything else to me, except that they regarded him as suspect on account of the propositions he held concerning the immobility of the sun and the motion of the earth, and because this man wants to interpret Holy Scripture against the common meaning of the Holy Fathers.

He added on his own: This man, together with others, belongs to an Academy—I do not know whether they organized it themselves—which has the title of "Lincean." And they correspond with others in Germany, at least Galileo does, as one sees from that book of his on sunspots.

Q: Whether he had been told himself in detail by Father Ferdinando Ximenes the persons from whom he learned about those propositions, that God is not a substance but an accident, that God is sensuous, and that the miracles of the Saints are not true miracles.

A: I seem to remember that he gave the name of Attavanti, whom I have described as one of those who uttered the said propositions. I do not remember any others.

Q: Where, when, in the presence of whom, and on what occasion Father Ferdinando related that Galilei's disciples had mentioned to him the said propositions.

A: It was on several occasions (sometimes in the cloister, sometimes in the dormitory, sometimes in his cell) that Father Ferdinando told me he had heard the said propositions from Galileo's disciples; he did this after I had preached that sermon, the occasion being that of telling me that he had defended me against these people. And I do not remember that there ever was anyone else present.

Q: About his hostility toward the said Galileo, toward the Attavanti character, and also toward other disciples of the said Galileo.

A: Not only do I not have any hostility toward the said Galileo, but I do not even know him. Similarly, I do not have any hostility or hatred toward Attavanti, or toward other disciples of Galileo. Rather I pray to God for them.

[311] Q: Whether the said Galileo teaches publicly in Florence, and what discipline; and whether his disciples are numerous.

A: I do not know whether Galileo lectures publicly, nor whether he has many disciples. I do know that in Florence he has many followers who are called Galileists. They are the ones who extol and praise his doctrine and opinions.

Q: What home town the said Galileo is from, what his profession is, and where he studied.

A: He regards himself as a Florentine, but I have heard that he is a Pisan. His profession is that of mathematician. As far as I have heard, he studied in Pisa and has lectured at Padua. He is past sixty years old.

With this he was dismissed, having been bound to silence by oath and his signature having been obtained.

I, Fra Tommaso Caccini, bear witness to the things said above.

§7. Inquisition Minutes (25 February 1616)[12]

The Most Illustrious Lord Cardinal Millini notified the Reverend Fathers Lord Assessor and Lord Commissary of the Holy Office that, after the report-ing of the judgment by the Father Theologians against the propositions of the mathematician Galileo (to the effect that the sun stands still at the center of the world and the earth moves even with the diurnal motion), His Holiness ordered the Most Illustrious Lord Cardinal Bellarmine to call Galileo before himself and warn him to abandon these opinions; and if he should refuse to obey, the Father Commissary, in the presence of a notary and witnesses, is to issue him an injunction to abstain completely from teaching or defending this doctrine and opinion or from discussing it; and further, if he should not acquiesce, he is to be imprisoned.

§8. Special Injunction (26 February 1616)[13]

[321] At the palace of the usual residence of the said Most Illustrious Lord Cardinal Bellarmine and in the chambers of His Most Illustrious Lordship, [322] and fully in the presence of the Reverend Father Michelangelo Segizzi of Lodi, O.P. and Commissary General of the Holy Office, having summoned the above-mentioned Galileo before himself, the same Most Illustrious Lord Cardinal warned Galileo that the above-mentioned opinion was erroneous and that he should abandon it; and thereafter, indeed immediately, before me and witnesses, the Most Illustrious Lord Cardinal himself being also present still, the aforesaid Father Commissary, in the name of His Holiness the Pope and of the whole Congregation of the Holy Office, ordered and enjoined the said Galileo, who was himself still present, to abandon completely the above-mentioned opinion that the sun stands still at the center of the world and the earth moves, and henceforth not to hold, teach, or defend it in any way whatever, either orally or in writing; otherwise the Holy Office would

---

12. Reprinted from Finocchiaro 1989, 147; cf. Galilei 1890–1909, 19: 321.
13. Reprinted from Finocchiaro 1989, 147–48; cf. Galilei 1890–1909, 19: 321–22.

start proceedings against him. The same Galileo acquiesced in this injunction and promised to obey.

Done in Rome at the place mentioned above, in the presence, as witnesses, of the Reverend Badino Nores of Nicosia in the kingdom of Cyprus, and of Agostino Mongardo from the Abbey of Rose in the diocese of Montepulciano, both belonging to the household of the said Most Illustrious Lord Cardinal.

§9. Inquisition Minutes (3 March 1616)[14]

The Most Illustrious Lord Cardinal Bellarmine having given the report that the mathematician Galileo Galilei had acquiesced when warned, on orders from the Holy Congregation,[15] to abandon the opinion which he held till then, to the effect that the sun stands still at the center of the spheres but that the earth is in motion; and the Decree of the Congregation of the Index having been presented, in which were prohibited and suspended, respectively, the writings of Nicolaus Copernicus *On the Revolutions of the Heavenly Spheres*, of Diego de Zúñiga *On Job*, and of the Carmelite Father Paolo Antonio Foscarini; His Holiness ordered that the edict of this suspension and prohibition, respectively, be published by the Master of the Sacred Palace.

§10. Index's Decree (5 March 1616)[16]

[322] Decree of the Holy Congregation of the Most Illustrious Lord Cardinals especially charged by His Holiness Pope Paul V and by the Holy Apostolic See with the Index of books and their licensing, prohibition, correction, and printing in all of Christendom. To be published everywhere.

In regard to several books containing various heresies and errors, to prevent the emergence of more serious harm throughout Christendom, the Holy Congregation of the Most Illustrious Lord Cardinals in charge of the Index has decided that they should be altogether condemned and prohibited, as indeed with the present decree it condemns and prohibits them, wherever and in whatever language they are printed or about to be printed. It orders that henceforth no one, of whatever station or condition, should dare print them, or have them printed, or read them, or have them in one's possession in any way, under penalty specified in the Holy Council of Trent and in the *Index*

---

14. Reprinted from Finocchiaro 1989, 148; cf. Galilei 1890–1909, 19: 278.
15. Here I have emended my earlier translation of this clause (Finocchiaro 1989, 148), thus following a suggestion by Speller (2008, 95).
16. Reprinted from Finocchiaro 1989, 148–50; cf. Galilei 1890–1909, 19: 322–23.

of Prohibited Books; and under the same penalty, whoever is now or will be in the future in possession of them is required to surrender them to ordinaries[17] or to inquisitors, immediately after learning of the present decree. The books are listed below:[18]

Calvinist Theology (in three parts), by Conradus Schlusserburgius.

Scotanus Redivivus, or Erotic Commentary in Three Parts, etc.

[323] *Historical Explanation of the Most Serious Question in the Christian Churches Especially in the West, from the Time of the Apostles All the Way to Our Age,* by Jacobus Usserius, professor of sacred theology at the Dublin Academy in Ireland.

Inquiry Concerning the Pre-eminence Among European Provinces, Conducted at the Illustrious College of Tübingen, in 1613 A.D., by Fridericus Achilles, Duke of Wittenberg.

Donellus's Principles, or Commentaries on Civil Law, Abridged so as…, etc, by Hugo Donellus.

This Holy Congregation has also learned about the spreading and acceptance by many of the false Pythagorean doctrine, altogether contrary to the Holy Scripture, that the earth moves and the sun is motionless, which is also taught by Nicolaus Copernicus's *On the Revolutions of the Heavenly Spheres* and by Diego de Zúñiga's *On Job.* This may be seen from a certain letter published by a certain Carmelite Father, whose title is *Letter of the Reverend Father Paolo Antonio Foscarini, on the Pythagorean and Copernican Opinion of the Earth's Motion and Sun's Rest and on the New Pythagorean World System* (Naples: Lazzaro Scoriggio, 1615), in which the said Father tries to show that the above-mentioned doctrine of the sun's rest at the center of the world and of the earth's motion is consonant with the truth and does not contradict Holy Scripture. Therefore, in order that this opinion may not advance any further to the prejudice of Catholic truth, the Congregation has decided that the books by Nicolaus Copernicus (*On the Revolutions of Spheres*) and by Diego de Zúñiga (*On Job*) be suspended until corrected; but that the book of the Carmelite Father Paolo Antonio Foscarini be completely prohibited and condemned; and that all other books which teach the same be likewise prohibited, according to whether with the present Decree it prohibits, condemns, and suspends them respectively. In witness thereof, this decree has been signed by the hand and stamped with the seal of the Most Illustrious and Reverend Lord Cardinal of Saint Cecilia,[19] Bishop of Albano, on 5 March 1616.

---

17. An "ordinary" would usually be a bishop.

18. For attempts to precisely identify these works and authors, see Mayaud 1997, 40 n. 8, 301–6; Mayer 2012, 99–100. Here I have limited myself to making a few minor emendations to Finocchiaro 1989, 149.

19. Paolo Sfondrati.

§11. Bellarmine's Certificate (26 May 1616)[20]

[348] We, Robert Cardinal Bellarmine, have heard that Mr. Galileo Galilei is being slandered or alleged to have abjured in our hands and also to have been given salutary penances for this. Having been sought about the truth of the matter, we say that the above-mentioned Galileo has not abjured in our hands, or in the hands of others here in Rome, or anywhere else that we know, any opinion or doctrine of his; nor has he received any penances, salutary or otherwise. On the contrary, he has only been notified of the declaration made by the Holy Father and published by the Sacred Congregation of the Index, whose content is that the doctrine attributed to Copernicus (that the earth moves around the sun and the sun stands at the center of the world without moving from east to west) is contrary to Holy Scripture and therefore cannot be defended or held.[21] In witness whereof we have written and signed this with our own hands, on this 26th day of May 1616.

---

20. Reprinted from Finocchiaro 1989, 153; cf. Galilei 1890–1909, 19: 348.
21. The content of this sentence should be compared and contrasted with that of the Index's Decree (§10) and with that of the Special Injunction (§8); many of the issues in the trial hinge on this.

CHAPTER 4

Reports and Responses:
Assimilation of Prohibition

§12. Guicciardini to Cosimo (4 March 1616)[1]

[241] Galileo gave more weight to his own opinion than to that of his friends: Lord Cardinal del Monte and I (to the small extent I was able to), as well as several cardinals of the Holy Office, [242] tried to persuade him to keep quiet and not to stir up this business; they pointed out that if he wanted to hold this opinion, he should hold it quietly, without making such an effort to encourage and draw others to hold it too; they all felt that his coming here was harmful and damaging to him, and that he behaved as if he was here not only to defend himself from his enemies but to receive some prize. For this he thought they were being cold toward his goal and his desires; thus, after having talked to and tired many cardinals, he sought the favor of Cardinal Orsini, and to this end he managed to obtain a very warm letter from Your Most Serene Highness for the cardinal.

At the consistory last Wednesday, this cardinal spoke to the pope in favor of the said Galileo, but I do not know how carefully and prudently. The pope told him that it would be good for Galileo to abandon this opinion. Orsini answered something to pressure the pope, who cut the discussion and told him that he would forward the issue to the Lord Cardinals of the Holy Office. After Orsini left, His Holiness met with Bellarmine and discussed this matter with him; they agreed that this opinion of Galileo was erroneous and heretical. The day before yesterday, I hear, there was a meeting about this matter, to declare it such; Copernicus, and other authors who have written about it, will be either emended and corrected, or prohibited; I think that Galileo personally cannot suffer because he will be prudent and will feel and want what the Holy Church feels and wants.

However, he gets inflamed with his opinions and feels very passionate about them; he does not have the fortitude and the prudence to be capable of prevailing. So this Roman sky is very dangerous for him, especially in this age when the ruler here abhors the *belles-lettres* and these intellects, and does not want to hear about these novelties and subtleties, and everyone tries to

---

1. Galilei 1890–1909, 12: 241–43 (no. 1185); newly translated by Finocchiaro.

accommodate one's brain and nature to his; thus, even those who have some knowledge and curiosity, if they are clever, appear to be the contrary of what they are, so as not to arouse suspicion and get into trouble. There are friars and others here who have ill will toward Galileo and who persecute him, and as I said, he is not at all attuned to this town; he could get himself and others involved in a great mess, and I do not see for what purpose and for what reason he came here and what he can gain by remaining. You know very well how the Most Serene House of Your Highness acted toward the Church of God on similar occasions in the past, in regard to persons and things touching the Holy Inquisition. I do not see why one should get involved in these difficulties and run these risks without a grave reason, when no benefit but great harm may result. If this is done only to please Galileo, it should be noted that he is very passionate about the matter, as if it were something personal, and he does not perceive or see what he should; thus, as has happened so far, he will be trapped without knowing and will endanger himself and anyone who will agree with his wishes or who will let himself be persuaded by him of the things he wants.

The Court here finds these things shameful and abhorrent; and if when the Lord Cardinal[2] comes here in accordance with ecclesiastic custom, he appears to oppose the deliberations of the Church and does not accept the will of the pope and of a Congregation such as that of the Holy Office, which is the foundation of religion and the most important one in Rome, he will lose a great deal and will cause great disgust. If in his [243] receptions and meetings he surrounds himself with men who are passionate and want to support and show off their opinions by means of struggle, especially regarding astrological or philosophical topics, everybody will run away because, as I said, here the pope is so averse to it that everyone tries to appear thick-headed and ignorant; thus, any men of letters that might come from there will be (I dare not say) harmful, but dangerous and of little use, and the less they show their learning the better, unless they do it with extreme discretion. If Galileo waits here for the Lord Cardinal and entangles him in this business in any way, the result will be very unpleasant; he is vehement, fixated, and passionate, so that it is impossible for anyone around him to escape from his clutches.

This situation is not a laughing matter and can become consequential and important (if it has not already become such), as the prudence of Your Most Serene Highness can understand very well; and this man is here at the house[3] of Your Most Serene Highness and of the Lord Cardinal and under their roof and protection, and he exploits your name; for these reasons, to discharge my

---

2. Carlo de' Medici (1595–1666), younger brother of Grand Duke Cosimo II.
3. Since his arrival in Rome in December 1615, Galileo had been lodging at Villa Medici, the magnificent palace owned by the Tuscan grand duke.

duties, I have wanted to relate to Your Most Serene Highness what has happened and what one hears about this matter.

§13. Galileo to Picchena (6 March 1616)[4]

I did not write to Your Most Illustrious Lordship at the time of the last postal delivery because there was nothing new to communicate to you, insofar as they were about to make a decision on that business which I mentioned to you as being of public interest, and which concerned me only because my enemies wanted to drag me into it at any cost. I am referring to the [244] deliberations by the Holy Church about Copernicus's book and his opinion on the earth's motion and sun's stability, which about a year ago was the subject of a complaint in Santa Maria Novella and then here in Rome on the part of the same friar,[5] who called it heretical and against the faith. Together with his followers, he tried orally and in writing to make this idea prevail, but events have shown that his effort did not find approval with the Holy Church. She has only decided that that opinion does not agree with the Holy Scriptures, and so only those books are prohibited which have explicitly maintained that it does not conflict with the Scripture.[6] There is only one such book, in the form of a letter by a Carmelite Father,[7] printed last year, and it alone is prohibited. Diego de Zúñiga, an Augustinian hermit who printed a book on Job thirty years ago and held that that opinion is not repugnant to the Scriptures, is suspended until corrected; and the correction is to remove from it a page in the commentary on the words "Who shaketh the earth out of her place, etc."[8] As for the book of Copernicus himself, ten lines will be removed from the Preface to Paul III, where he mentions that he does not think such a doctrine is repugnant to the Scriptures; as I understand it, they could remove a word here and there, where two or three times he calls the earth a star.[9] The correction of these two books has been assigned to Lord Cardinal Caetani. There is no mention of other authors.

---

4. Reprinted from Finocchiaro 1989, 150–51; cf. Galilei 1890–1909, 12: 243–45 (no. 1187).
5. Tommaso Caccini.
6. In the last two sentences, Galileo makes the important and valid distinction between heresy and contrariety to Scripture; in order to be heretical, an idea that is contrary to Scripture must also be contrary to an explicit and official proclamation by the Church addressed to all who have been baptized. Cf. Finocchiaro 2005, 272–74; 2010, 205–6.
7. Paolo Antonio Foscarini.
8. Job 9:6.
9. Such corrections were made a few years thereafter, and were published by the Index on 15 May 1620. See Galilei 1890–1909, 19: 400–401; Finocchiaro 1989, 200–202.

As one can see from the very nature of the business, I am not mentioned, nor would I have gotten involved in it if, as I said, my enemies had not dragged me into it. What I have done on the matter can always be seen from my writings pertaining to it, which I save in order to be able to shut the mouth of malicious gossipers at any time, and because I can show that my behavior in this affair has been such that a saint would not have handled it either with greater reverence or with greater zeal toward the Holy Church. This perhaps has not been done by my enemies, who have not refrained from any machination, calumny, and diabolical suggestion, as their Most Serene Highnesses and also Your Lordship will hear at length in due course. Furthermore, experience has in many ways made me grasp how much reason I had to fear some persons' dislike of me, [245] which I think I mentioned to you, and so I can believe that the same feeling will make them alter the story when they relate it; therefore, I beg Your Lordship, if need be, to keep for me until my return the regard which my sincerity deserves. At any rate, I am very sure that the coming here of the Most Illustrious and Most Reverend Lord Cardinal[10] will relieve me of the need to say even a word, such is the reputation I enjoy everywhere at this Court. Above all, Your Lordship will learn with how much calmness and moderation I have behaved, and how respectful I have been of the reputation of those who, on the contrary, very sharply and without any reservation have always sought the destruction of mine; you will be surprised. I say this to Your Very Illustrious Lordship in case you hear something which would make me look worse, for it would be absolutely most false, as I hope you will learn from other more reliable sources.

As for my trip to Naples, so far the weather and the roads have been abominable; if they improve, I shall see what I can do, for I want to give top priority, over any other business of mine, to my being here when the Lord Cardinal arrives. In the meantime, I am grateful for the benevolence of their Most Serene Highnesses; I am also infinitely obliged to you, as my irreplaceable patron and protector, and I reverently kiss your hands.

§14. Sarpi's Legal Opinion (7 May 1616)[11]

I have seen the decree of the Roman Congregation for the Index of books, submitted to the Most Excellent College by the Most Illustrious Lord Count Dal Zaffo, Expert Councillor on Heresy. In accordance with the order of Your Serenity, and speaking with reverence, I will say this.

---

10. Carlo de' Medici.
11. In Berti 1876, 151–53; newly translated by Finocchiaro. For more details, see Finocchiaro 2005, 70–72.

That decree contains two parts. The first is a prohibition of five books by Protestant authors recently printed on the other side of the Alps: two of them contain only doctrines that are heretical and contrary to the holy faith; the other three, although they do not treat mainly of religion, nevertheless contain many heretical doctrines. Thus, one can be sure that prohibiting them is a service to God and contributes to the conservation of the purity of the holy religion.

The second part of the decree is the suspension of a book by the famous astronomer Nicolaus Copernicus, and furthermore the prohibition of a letter printed in Naples on the same subject by another author who follows his doctrine. Nicolaus Copernicus was a Catholic clergyman, a lecturer at the University of Rome, and a close acquaintance of Pope Paul III (God bless his soul) when he was a cardinal and also after he became pope; his book was printed slightly less than 100 years ago and was seen and read by all Europe with the judgment that its author was the most learned professional astronomer that the world has ever had; indeed the reform of the calendar made by Pope Gregory XIII was based on his doctrine. For these reasons, the suspension of the book is bound to cause puzzlement for the novel practice of suspending an old book seen by the whole world and previously uncensored either by the Council of Trent or by Rome. On the other hand, we must consider that this kind of doctrine does not touch in any way the power of the state and does not provide any benefit to temporal authority; nor does it affect the art of printing in this state, for it is certain that none of these books have ever been printed in Venice (but rather in Rome); and even if they had ever been printed here with the proper license, there may be important reasons for allowing prohibition. In any case, since the persons who practice the profession of astronomer are very few, one need not fear that a scandal can emerge. Therefore, I would judge that to allow the prohibition and the suspension for these three[12] other books cannot cause any public harm.

However, I would point out with reverence that if the prohibition were to be published without receiving a public endorsement, it would do considerable harm to the concordat reached between the Apostolic See and the Most Serene Republic in 1596 on the matter of the prohibition of books; and for innumerable and extremely important reasons, it is right and necessary to keep it alive with every diligent care. Thus, it would be a public disservice if the Roman decree were published and promulgated in Venice by the Father Inquisitor or other clergyman, after the merely oral approval of the Most Illustrious Lords Expert Councillors [on Heresy], as I believe the Father Inquisitor plans to do. Instead, for the preservation of the public interest I

---

12. Sarpi did not actually mention the third book, Diego de Zúñiga's *Commentaries on Job*.

would deem it necessary to have a meeting of the Office of the Inquisition and the [State] Council [on Heresy] for the purpose of compiling a decree that would state substantially this: that on such and such a date there was a meeting of the Office of the Inquisition and such and such Most Illustrious Lords Councillors; that such and such a decree of the Roman Congregation of the Index was examined and read; and that it was decided to publish it. This action should be recorded in the book of public proceedings of the Office of the Inquisition; and if the Father Inquisitor should want to print in Venice the Roman decree, he should not be allowed unless he adds the above-mentioned Venetian decree; thus, anyone seeing the Roman prohibition would simultaneously see the endorsement given by the representatives of the public, and the concordat will be respected.[13] I submit my opinion to the sublime wisdom of Your Serenity.

§15. Galileo to Cioli (7 March 1631)[14]

As Your Most Illustrious Lordship knows, I was in Rome to get a license for my *Dialogue* and have it printed and published, and so I delivered it into the hands of the Most Reverend Father Master of the Sacred Palace.[15] He commissioned his comrade Father Fra Raffaello Visconti to examine it with the greatest care, and to note whether he had any misgivings about it or whether it contained any ideas to be corrected. The latter did that very strictly, as I too asked him to do. [216] While I was applying for the license and for the personal endorsement of the same Father Master, His Most Reverend Paternity decided that he wanted to read it again himself. He did this and returned the book licensed and endorsed by his own signature, so that after a two months' stay in Rome I returned to Florence.

However, I was thinking of sending the book back there after I had completed the table of contents, the dedication, and other things; it would have been handed over to the Most Illustrious and Distinguished Lord Prince Cesi, head of the Lincean Academy, to take care of the printing, as he had been in the habit of doing for other works of mine and by other Academicians. There followed the death of the same Prince, as well as the suspension of commerce,[16] so that printing the work in Rome was hindered.

---

13. As far as I know, the procedure recommended by Sarpi was never followed, and so perhaps the anti-Copernican decree of the Index was never legally valid in the Venetian Republic. The situation was analogous in France; cf. Finocchiaro 2005, 66.

14. Reprinted from Finocchiaro 1989, 206–9; cf. Galilei 1890–1909, 14: 215–18 (no. 2115).

15. Niccolò Riccardi.

16. Due to an outbreak of the plague.

Thus, I made the decision to have it printed here; I found a suitable publisher and printer; and we made the necessary agreements. For this I also got a license here from the Most Reverend Vicar, the Most Reverend Inquisitor, and the Most Illustrious Lord Niccolò Antella. Since I thought it proper to inform the Father Master in Rome about what was happening, and about the obstacles hindering its printing in Rome in accordance with the intention I had expressed to him, I wrote to His Most Reverend Paternity that I was thinking of printing it here. By way of the Most Distinguished Ladyship wife[17] of the ambassador, he let me know that he wanted to give another look at the work and that therefore I should send him a copy. Then, as you know, I came to Your Most Illustrious Lordship to find out whether at that time such a large volume could have been sent to Rome safely, and you told me clearly No, and that simple letters were barely going through safely. So I wrote again, informing him of such an obstacle, and offering to send the book's preface and ending; there, the authorities could add or remove at will and insert all the qualifications they wanted, since I would not refuse giving these thoughts of mine the labels of chimeras, dreams, paralogisms, and empty images, and since I would always defer and submit everything to the absolute wisdom and indubitable doctrines of the higher sciences, etc.; as for reviewing the work again, this could be done here by a person acceptable to His Most Reverend Paternity. He agreed to this, and I sent the work's preface and ending. He settled on the very Reverend Father Fra Giacinto Stefani, consultant to the Inquisition, as the new reviewer; the latter reviewed the entire work with the greatest accuracy and severity (as I also asked him to do), noticing even some minutiae [217] which should not cause a shadow of a scruple even to my most malicious enemy, let alone to himself. Indeed, His Paternity has stated that at more than one place in my book tears came to his eyes when seeing with how much humility and reverent submission I defer to the authority of superiors, and he acknowledges (as also do all those who have read the book) that I should be begged to publish such a work, rather than being hindered in many ways which I need not list for now.

Some months ago Father Benedetto Castelli wrote to me that he had met the Most Reverend Father Master several times, and heard from him that he was about to return the above-mentioned preface and ending, revised to his complete satisfaction; but this has never happened, and I no longer feel like mentioning the matter. In the meantime the work stays in a corner, and my life is wasted as I continue living in constant ill health.

---

17. Caterina Riccardi Niccolini (1598–1676), who happened to be a cousin of the Master of the Sacred Palace.

So yesterday I came to Florence, first on orders from the Most Serene Patron[18] to see the drawings of the Cathedral's façade, and then to appeal to his kindness. I wanted to let him hear about the state of this business, and to ask him to arrange, with the advice of Your Most Illustrious Lordship, that at least we may understand clearly the feelings of the Most Reverend Father Master; furthermore, if you both agreed, Your Most Illustrious Lordship with the approval of His Highness could have written to the Most Distinguished Lord Ambassador to speak with the Father Master, conveying to him His Highness's desire that this business be brought to an end, in part to know what kind of man His Highness employs in his service. However, not only was I unable to speak with His Highness, but also I could not stay to look at the drawings, because I became very sick. Just now a messenger from Court came here to find out about my condition, which is such that I really should not have gotten out of bed were it not for the opportunity and desire to mention this business of mine to Your Most Illustrious Lordship. So I beg you to do me the favor of accomplishing what I was unable to do yesterday, by following the above-mentioned plan and bringing about, in the appropriate ways you know better than I, the resolution of this affair, so that while I am still alive I may know the outcome of my long and hard work.

[218] Your Most Illustrious Lordship will receive this from the hand of the above-mentioned messenger, and I shall eagerly wait to hear from Mr. Geri[19] what Your Most Illustrious Lordship has decided about this. Now I reverently kiss your hands and pray for your happiness. Finally, since His Most Serene Highness is kind enough to show his worry about my condition, Your Most Illustrious Lordship can explain to him that I should get by reasonably well if I were not afflicted with mental disturbances.

§16. Riccardi to Florentine Inquisitor (24 May 1631)[20]

Mr. Galilei is thinking of publishing there a work of his, formerly entitled *On the Ebb and Flow of the Sea*, in which he discusses in a probable fashion the Copernican system and motion of the earth, and he attempts to facilitate the understanding of that great natural mystery by means of this supposition, corroborating it in turn because of this usefulness.[21] He came to Rome to show us

---

18. Ferdinando II de' Medici (1610–1670), who had become grand duke upon the premature death in 1621 of his father, Cosimo II.

19. Geri Bocchineri (d. 1650), private secretary to the grand duke, and distant relative of Galileo.

20. Reprinted from Finocchiaro 1989, 212; cf. Galilei 1890–1909, 19: 327.

21. This interpretation of Galileo's *Dialogue* is essentially correct, and importantly so. Cf. the Introduction (§0.6) above; and Finocchiaro 2014, 45–46, 243–58.

the work, which I endorsed, with the understanding that certain adjustments would be made to it and shown back to us to receive the final approval for printing. As this cannot be done due to current restrictions on the roads and the risks for the manuscript, and since the author wants to finalize the business there, Your Very Reverend Paternity can avail yourself of your authority and dispatch or not dispatch the book without depending in any way on my review.

However, I want to remind you that Our Master[22] thinks that the title and subject should not focus on the ebb and flow but absolutely on the mathematical examination of the Copernican position on the earth's motion, with the aim of proving that, if we remove divine revelation and sacred doctrine, the appearances could be saved with this supposition; one would thus be answering all the contrary indications which may be put forth by experience and by Peripatetic[23] philosophy, so that one would never be admitting the absolute truth of this opinion, but only its hypothetical truth without the benefit of Scripture. It must also be shown that this work is written only to show that we do know all the arguments that can be advanced for this side, and that it was not for lack of knowledge that the decree[24] was issued in Rome; this should be the gist of the book's beginning and ending, which I will send from here properly revised. With this provision the book will encounter no obstacle here in Rome, and Your Very Reverend Paternity will be able to please the author and serve the Most Serene Highness, who shows so much concern in this matter. I remind you that I am your servant and I beg you to honor me with your commands.

§17. Niccolini to Cioli (5 September 1632)[25]

Yesterday I did not have the time to report to Your Most Illustrious Lordship what had transpired (in a very emotional atmosphere) between myself and the Pope in regard to Mr. Galilei's work. I appreciated the opportunity because I was able to say certain things to His Holiness himself, though without any profit. As for me, I too am beginning to believe, as Your Most Illustrious Lordship well expresses it, that the sky is about to fall.

---

22. *Nostro Signore*, literally "Our Lord," meaning Pope Urban VIII.
23. *Peripatetic* was a nickname given to Aristotelians, stemming from a Greek word that means literally someone who walks around; they acquired this nickname because in the school founded by Aristotle the teachers had the habit of walking around while lecturing.
24. The Index's Decree of 5 March 1616 (§10).
25. Reprinted from Finocchiaro 1989, 229–32; cf. Galilei 1890–1909, 14: 383–85 (no. 2298).

While we were discussing those delicate subjects of the Holy Office, His Holiness exploded into great anger, and suddenly he told me that even our Galilei had dared entering where he should not have, into the most serious and dangerous subjects which could be stirred up at this time. I replied that Mr. Galilei had not published without the approval of his ministers, and that for that purpose I myself had obtained and sent the prefaces to your city. He answered, with the same outburst of rage, that he had been deceived by Galileo and Ciampoli; that in particular Ciampoli had dared tell him that Mr. Galilei was ready to do all His Holiness ordered and everything was fine; and that this was what he had been told, without having ever seen or read the work. He also complained about the Master of the Sacred Palace, although he said that the latter himself had been deceived: by having his written endorsement of the book pulled out of his hands with beautiful words; by the book being then printed in Florence on the basis of other endorsements, but without complying with the form given to [384] the Inquisitor; and by having his name printed in the book's list of imprimaturs, even though he has no jurisdiction over publications in other cities. Here I interjected that I knew His Holiness had appointed a commission for this purpose, and that, because it might have members who hate Mr. Galilei (as it does), I humbly begged His Holiness to agree to give him the opportunity to justify himself. His Holiness answered that in these matters of the Holy Office the procedure was simply to arrive at a censure and then call the defendant to recant. I replied: Does it thus not seem to Your Holiness that Galileo should know in advance the difficulties and the objections or the censures which are being raised against his work, and what the Holy Office is worried about? He answered violently: I say to Your Lordship that the Holy Office does not do these things and does not proceed this way, that these things are never given in advance to anyone, that such is not the custom; besides, he knows very well where the difficulties lie, if he wants to know them, since we have discussed them with him and he has heard them from ourselves. I replied begging him to consider that the book was explicitly dedicated to our Most Serene Patron and that they were dealing with one of his present employees, and saying that because of this too I hoped he would be helpful and would also order his ministers to take it into consideration. He said that he had prohibited works which had his pontifical name in front and were dedicated to himself, and that in such matters, involving great harm to religion (indeed the worst ever conceived), His Highness too should contribute to preventing it, being a Christian prince; furthermore, that because of this, I should clearly write to the Most Serene Highness to be careful not to get involved as he had in the other case of [Mariano] Alidosi, because he would not come out of it honorably. I retorted that I was sure I would receive orders to trouble him again, and that I would do it, but that I did not believe His Holiness would bring about the prohibition of the already approved book without at least hearing Mr. Galilei first. His Holiness answered that this was the least ill which could be done to him, and that he should take care not to be summoned by the Holy Office; that he has appointed a commission of theologians and other persons versed in various sciences, serious and of holy mind, who are weighing every minutia, word for word, since one is dealing with the most perverse subject one could ever come across; and again that his complaint was to have been deceived by Galileo and Ciampoli. Finally, he told me to write to our Most Serene Patron that the doctrine is extremely perverse, that they would review everything with seriousness, and that His Highness should not get involved but should go slow; furthermore, not only did he impose on me the secret about what he had just told me, but he charged me to report that he also was imposing it on His Highness. He added that he has used every civility with Mr. Galilei, since he explained to the latter what he knows; since he has not sent the case to the Congregation of the Holy Inquisition, as is the norm, but rather to a special commission newly created, which is something; and since he has used better manners with Galileo than the latter has used with His Holiness, who was deceived. Thus I had an unpleasant meeting, and I feel the Pope could not have a worse disposition toward our poor Mr. Galilei. Your Most Illustrious Lordship can imagine in what condition I returned home yesterday morning.

This past Monday I had gone to meet with the Master of the Sacred Palace. After explaining to him all the points from your letter, and after also calming him in regard to his complaints, I gathered some hopeful signs rather than anything else; [385] in particular, he seemed to believe that one would not go as far as prohibiting the book, but that it would only be corrected and emended in some things, which are really bad. He also said that if he could tell me something in advance, without detriment to him and without disobeying orders, he would do it; but that he too had to move cautiously since he had already gone through storms in this regard and he had helped himself as well as he knew how. He complains that the form given in his letter to the Inquisitor was not observed; that the declaration to be printed at the beginning is in a different typeface and is not linked to the rest of the work; and that the ending does not correspond to the beginning at all.

As for me, if I have to express my sense to Your Most Illustrious Lordship, I believe it is necessary to take this business without violence, and to deal with the ministers and with the Lord Cardinal Barberini rather than with the Pope himself, for when His Holiness gets something into his head, that is the end of the matter, especially if one is opposing, threatening, or defying him, since then he hardens and shows no respect to anyone. The best course is to temporize and to try to move him by persistent, skillful, and quiet diplomacy, involving also his ministers, depending on the nature of the business. For example, in the case of Mr. Mariano [Alidosi] we should have tried to convince the nuncio and have him do the writing and the pleading, without us entering into the merits of the case and especially without us writing briefs; these may have given him the opportunity to show that he was very learned and knew more than our experts, and to give contrary advice; if we had done that, we would not have exacerbated the feelings of the Pope, to whom one must not give indication of wanting to dispute the administration of justice.

The strong letter which Your Most Illustrious Lordship wrote on the 30th in regard to Mr. Galilei, and which I have just now received, does not seem well balanced to me now that I have heard the Pope, since by making an uproar we will exasperate and spoil the situation. However, I must only obey, because my will should depend entirely on the orders of the Patrons. This is really going to be a troublesome affair. I am thinking of again going to talk with the Master of the Sacred Palace, to tell him some of what I gathered from His Holiness, as well as to hear what he thinks of it and what his attitude is now. However, the matter proceeds with extreme secrecy. Finally, I express my reverence to Your Most Illustrious Lordship.

§18. Niccolini to Cioli (27 February 1633)[26]

Yesterday morning I explained to His Holiness what Your Most Illustrious Lordship had instructed me to say in regard to the alliance which could be made at this time against the Turks...

I informed him of Mr. Galileo's arrival,[27] adding that I hoped His Holiness was convinced of his reverent and most devout observance in ecclesiastical matters, and especially in the matter at hand; for he had come in very high spirits and resolved to submit entirely to his wise judgment and to the most prudent views of the Congregation, and he had even uplifted and consoled me. His Holiness answered that he had done Mr. Galilei a singular favor, not done to others, by allowing him to stay in this house rather than at the Holy Office, and that this kind procedure had been used only because he is a dear employee of the Most Serene Patron and because of the regard due to His Highness; for a Knight of the House of Gonzaga, son of Ferdinando, had been not only placed in a litter and escorted to Rome under guard, but taken to the Castle and kept there for a long time till the end of the trial. I showed myself to be aware of the nature of the favor, and I humbly thanked His Holiness; then I begged him to give orders for expediting the trial, so that [56] the sick old man could return home as soon as possible. He replied that

---

26. Reprinted from Finocchiaro 1989, 245–46; cf. Galilei 1890–1909, 15: 55–56 (no. 2428).
27. Complying with the Inquisition's summons to Rome for trial, Galileo had arrived there on 13 February 1633.

the activities of the Holy Office ordinarily proceeded slowly, and that he did not really know whether one could hope for such a quick conclusion, since they were in the process of preparing for the formal proceedings and had not yet finished with that. Then he went on to say that, in short, Mr. Galilei had been ill-advised to publish these opinions of his, and it was the sort of thing for which Ciampoli was responsible; for, although he claims to want to discuss the earth's motion hypothetically, nevertheless, when he presents the arguments for it, he mentions and discusses it assertively and conclusively; furthermore, he had also violated the order given to him in 1616 by the Lord Cardinal Bellarmine in the name of the Congregation of the Index. In his defense I replied saying everything I remembered him expressing and explaining to me on this and related matters; but, as the subject is delicate and troublesome, and as His Holiness gives the impression that Mr. Galileo's doctrine is bad and that he even believes it, the task is not easy. Furthermore, even if they should be satisfied with his answers, they will not want to give the appearance of having made a blunder, after everybody knows they summoned him to Rome.

I strongly recommended him to the protection of the Lord Cardinal Barberini, and I did this all the more gladly inasmuch as I felt I found His Holiness less irritated than usual. His Eminence replied that he felt warmly toward Mr. Galilei and regarded him as an exceptional man, but that this subject is very delicate; for it involves the possibility of introducing some imaginary dogma into the world, particularly into Florence where (as I know) the intellects are very subtle and curious, and especially by his reporting much more validly what favors the side of the earth's motion than what can be adduced for the other side. I said that perhaps the nature of the situation indicated this, and therefore he was not to blame; but His Eminence answered that I was aware that I knew how to express exquisitely and how to justify wonderfully whatever he wanted.[28] Finally, I kiss your hands.

---

28. The issue expressed in the last two sentences is extremely important. For details and references, see Finocchiaro 2010, 242–43; 2011; 2014, 255–58, 322.

CHAPTER 5

Later Proceedings:
Condemnation of Galileo

§19. Special Commission Report on the
Dialogue (September 1632)[1]

[§19.1] In accordance with the order of Your Holiness, we have laid out the whole series of events pertaining to the printing of Galilei's book, which printing then took place in Florence. In essence the affair developed this way.

In the year 1630, Galileo took his book manuscript to the Father Master of the Sacred Palace in Rome, in order to have it reviewed for printing. The Father Master gave it for review to Father Raffaello Visconti, a friend of his and a professor of mathematics, who after several emendations was ready to give his approval as usual, if the book were to be printed in Rome.

We have written the said Father to send the said certificate, and we are now waiting for it. We have also written to get the original manuscript, in order to see the corrections made.

The Master of the Sacred Palace wanted to review the book himself; but, in order to shorten the time and to facilitate negotiations with printers, he stipulated that it be shown him page by page, and gave it the imprimatur for Rome.

Then the author went back to Florence and petitioned the Father Master for permission to print it in that city, which permission was denied. But the latter forwarded the case to the Inquisitor of Florence, thus removing himself from the transaction. Moreover, the Father Master notified the Inquisitor of what was required for publication, leaving to him the task of having it printed or not.

The Master of the Sacred Palace has shown a copy of the letter he wrote the Inquisitor about this business, as well as a copy of the Inquisitor's reply to the said [325] Master of the Sacred Palace. In it the Inquisitor says that he gave the manuscript for correction to Father Stefani, consultant to the Holy Office.

After this the Master of the Sacred Palace did not hear anything, except that he saw the book printed in Florence and published with the Inquisitor's imprimatur, and that there is also an imprimatur for Rome.

---

1. Reprinted from Finocchiaro 1989, 218–22; cf. Galilei 1890–1909, 19: 324–27.

We think that Galileo may have overstepped his instructions by asserting absolutely the earth's motion and the sun's immobility, and thus deviating from hypothesis; that he may have wrongly attributed the existing ebb and flow of the sea to the nonexistent immobility of the sun and motion of the earth, which are the main things; and that he may have been deceitfully silent about an injunction given him by the Holy Office in the year 1616, whose tenor is: "that he abandon completely the above-mentioned opinion that the sun is the center of the world and the earth moves, nor henceforth hold, teach, or defend it in any way whatever, orally or in writing; otherwise the Holy Office would start proceedings against him. He acquiesced in this injunction and promised to obey."

One must now consider how to proceed, both against the person and concerning the printed book.

[§19.2] In point of fact:

1. Galilei did come to Rome in the year 1630, and he brought and showed his original manuscript to be reviewed for printing. Though he had been ordered to discuss the Copernican system only as a pure mathematical hypothesis, one found immediately that the book was not like this, but that it spoke absolutely, presenting the reasons for and against, though without deciding. Thus the Master of the Sacred Palace determined that the book be reviewed and be changed to the hypothetical mode: it should have a preface to which the body would conform, which would describe this manner of proceeding, and which would prescribe it to the whole dispute to follow, including the part against the Ptolemaic system, carried on merely *ad hominem* and to show that in reproving the Copernican system the Holy Congregation had heard all the arguments.

2. To follow this through, the book was given for review with these orders to Father Raffaello Visconti, a friend of the Master of the Sacred Palace, since he was a professor of mathematics. He reviewed it and emended it in many places, informing the Master about others disputed with the author, which the Master took out without further discussion. Having approved it for the rest, Father Visconti was ready to give it his endorsement to be placed at the beginning of the book as usual, if the book were to be printed in Rome as it was then presumed.

We have written the Inquisitor to send this endorsement to us and are expecting to receive it momentarily, and we have also sent for the original so that we can see the corrections made.

3. The Master of the Sacred Palace wanted to review the book himself, but, since the author complained about the unusual practice of a second revision and about the delay, to facilitate the process it was decided that before sending it to press the Master would see it page by page. In the meantime, to enable the author to negotiate with printers, he [326] was given the imprimatur for

Rome, the book's beginning was compiled, and printing was expected to begin soon.

4. The author then went back to Florence, and after a certain period he petitioned to print it in that city. The Master of the Sacred Palace absolutely denied the request, answering by saying that the original should be brought back to him to make the last revision agreed upon, and that without this he for his part would have never given permission to print it. The reply was that the original could not be sent because of the dangers of loss and the plague. Nevertheless, after the intervention of His Highness there, it was decided that the Master of the Sacred Palace would remove himself from the case and refer it to the Inquisitor of Florence: the Master would describe to him what was required for the correction of the book and would leave him the decision to print it or not, so that he would be using his authority, without any responsibility on the part of the Master's office. Accordingly, he wrote to the Inquisitor the letter whose copy is appended here, labeled A, dated 24 May 1631, received and acknowledged by the Inquisitor with the letter labeled B, where he says he entrusted the book to Father Stefani, consultant to the Holy Office there.

Then a brief composition of the book's preface was sent to the Inquisitor, so that the author would incorporate it with the whole, would embellish it in his own way, and would make the ending of the *Dialogue* conform with it. A copy of the sketch that was sent is enclosed labeled C, and a copy of the accompanying letter is enclosed labeled D.

5. After this the Master of the Sacred Palace was no longer involved in the matter, except when, the book having been printed and published without his knowledge, he received the first few copies and held them in customs, seeing that the instructions had not been followed. Then, upon orders from Our Ruler, he had them all seized where it was not too late and diligence made it possible to do so.

6. Moreover, there are in the book the following things to consider, as specific items of indictment:

i. That he used the imprimatur for Rome without permission and without sharing the fact of the book's being published with those who are said to have granted it.

ii. That he had the preface printed with a different type and rendered it useless by its separation from the body of the work; and that he put the "medicine of the end" in the mouth of a fool and in a place where it can only be found with difficulty, and then he had it approved coldly by the other speaker by merely mentioning but not elaborating the positive things he seems to utter against his will.

iii. That many times in the work there is a lack of and deviation from hypothesis, either by asserting absolutely the earth's motion and the sun's immobility, or by characterizing the supporting arguments as demonstrative and necessary, or by treating the negative side as impossible.

iv. He treats the issue as undecided and as if one should await rather than presuppose the resolution.

[327] v. The mistreatment of contrary authors and those most used by the Holy Church.

vi. That he wrongly asserts and declares a certain equality between the human and the divine intellect in the understanding of geometrical matters.

vii. That he gives as an argument for the truth the fact that Ptolemaics occasionally become Copernicans, but the reverse never happens.

viii. That he wrongly attributed the existing ebb and flow of the sea to the nonexistent immobility of the sun and motion of the earth.

All these things could be emended if the book were judged to have some utility which would warrant such a favor.

7. In 1616 the author had from the Holy Office the injunction "that he abandon completely the above-mentioned opinion that the sun is the center of the world and the earth moves, nor henceforth hold, teach, or defend it in any way, orally or in writing; otherwise the Holy Office would start proceedings against him. He acquiesced in this injunction and promised to obey."

§20. Galileo's First Deposition (12 April 1633)[2]

Summoned, there appeared personally in Rome at the palace of the Holy Office, in the usual quarters of the Reverend Father Commissary, fully in the presence of the Reverend Father Fra Vincenzo Maculano da Firenzuola, [337] Commissary General, and of his assistant Reverend Father Carlo Sinceri, Prosecutor of the Holy Office, etc.

Galileo, son of the late Vincenzio Galilei, Florentine, seventy years old, who, having taken a formal oath to tell the truth, was asked by the Fathers the following:

Q:[3] By what means and how long ago did he come to Rome.

A: I arrived in Rome the first Sunday of Lent, and I came in a litter.

Q: Whether he came of his own accord, or was called, or was ordered by someone to come to Rome, and by whom.

A: In Florence the Father Inquisitor ordered me to come to Rome and present myself to the Holy Office, this being an injunction by the officials of the Holy Office.

---

2. Reprinted from Finocchiaro 1989, 256–62; cf. Galilei 1890–1909, 19: 336–42.
3. Here and in other depositions, the questions are recorded as *indirect* queries, so that the letter Q ought to be taken to mean "He was asked," rather than simply "Question."

Q: Whether he knows or can guess the reason why he was ordered to come to Rome.

A: I imagine that the reason why I have been ordered to present myself to the Holy Office in Rome is to account for my recently printed book. I imagine this because of the injunction to the printer and to myself, a few days before I was ordered to come to Rome, not to issue any more of these books, and similarly because the printer was ordered by the Father Inquisitor to send the original manuscript of my book to the Holy Office in Rome.

Q: That he explain the character of the book on account of which he thinks he was ordered to come to Rome.

A: It is a book written in dialogue form, and it treats of the constitution of the world, that is, of the two chief systems, and of the arrangement of the heavens and the elements.

Q: Whether, if he were shown the said book, he is prepared to identify it as his.

A: I hope so; I hope that if the book is shown me I shall recognize it.

And having been shown one of the books printed in Florence in 1632, whose title is *Dialogue of Galileo Galilei Lincean . . . in Which One Examines the Two Systems of the World*, and having looked at it and inspected it carefully, he said: I know this book very well; it is one of those printed in Florence; and I acknowledge it as mine and written by me.

Q: Whether he likewise acknowledges each and every thing contained in the said book as his.

A: I know this book shown to me, for it is one of those printed in Florence; and I acknowledge all it contains as having been written by me.

Q: When and where he composed the said book, and how long it took him.

[338] A: In regard to the place, I composed it in Florence, beginning ten or twelve years ago; and it must have taken me seven or eight years, but not continuously.

Q: Whether he was in Rome other times, especially in the year 1616, and for what occasion.

A: I was in Rome in the year 1616; then I was here in the second year of His Holiness Urban VIII's pontificate; and lastly I was here three years ago, the occasion being that I wanted to have my book printed. The occasion for my being in Rome in the year 1616 was that, having heard objections to Nicolaus Copernicus's opinion on the earth's motion, the sun's stability, and the arrangement of the heavenly spheres, in order to be sure of holding only holy and Catholic opinions, I came to hear what was proper to hold in regard to this topic.

Q: Whether he came of his own accord or was summoned, what the reason was why he was summoned, and with which person or persons he discussed the above-mentioned topics.

A: In 1616 I came to Rome of my own accord, without being summoned, for the reason I mentioned. In Rome I discussed this matter with some cardinals who oversaw the Holy Office at that time, especially with Cardinals Bellarmine, Aracoeli, San Eusebio, Bonsi, and d'Ascoli.

Q: What specifically he discussed with the above-mentioned cardinals.

A: The occasion for discussing with the said cardinals was that they wanted to be informed about Copernicus's doctrine, his book being very difficult to understand for those who are not professional mathematicians and astronomers. In particular they wanted to understand the arrangement of the heavenly spheres according to Copernicus's hypothesis, how he places the sun at the center of the planets' orbits, how around the sun he places next the orbit of Mercury, around the latter that of Venus, then the moon around the earth, and around this Mars, Jupiter, and Saturn; and in regard to motion, he makes the sun stationary at the center and the earth turn on itself and around the sun, that is, on itself with the diurnal motion and around the sun with the annual motion.

Q: Since, as he says, he came to Rome to be able to have the resolution and the truth regarding the above, what then was decided about this matter.

A: Regarding the controversy which centered on the above-mentioned opinion of the sun's stability and earth's motion, it was decided by the Holy Congregation of the Index that this opinion, taken absolutely, is repugnant to Holy Scripture, and that it is to be admitted only suppositionally, in the way that Copernicus takes it.

Q: Whether he was then notified of the said decision, and by whom.

A: I was indeed notified of the said decision of the Congregation of the Index, and I was notified by Lord Cardinal Bellarmine.

Q: What the Most Eminent Bellarmine told him about the said decision, whether he said anything else about the matter, and if so what.

[339] A: Lord Cardinal Bellarmine told me that Copernicus's opinion could be held suppositionally, as Copernicus himself had held it. His Eminence knew that I held it suppositionally, namely in the way that Copernicus held it, as you can see from an answer by the same Lord Cardinal to a letter of Father Master Paolo Antonio Foscarini, Provincial of the Carmelites; I have a copy of this, and in it one finds these words: "I say that it seems to me that Your Paternity and Mr. Galileo are proceeding prudently by limiting yourselves to speaking suppositionally and not absolutely." This letter by the said Lord Cardinal is dated 12 April 1615. Moreover, he told me that otherwise, namely taken absolutely, the opinion could be neither held nor defended.

Q: What was decided and then made known to him precisely in the month of February 1616.

A: In the month of February 1616, Lord Cardinal Bellarmine told me that since Copernicus's opinion, taken absolutely, was contrary to Holy Scripture, it could be neither held nor defended, but that it could be taken and used suppositionally. In conformity with this I keep a certificate by Lord Cardinal Bellarmine himself, dated 26 May 1616, in which he says that Copernicus's opinion cannot be held or defended, being against Holy Scripture. I present a copy of this certificate, and here it is.

And he showed a sheet of paper with twelve lines of writing on one side only, beginning "We Robert Cardinal Bellarmine have" and ending "on this 26th day of May 1616," signed "The same mentioned above, Robert Cardinal Bellarmine." This evidence was accepted and marked with the letter *B*.

Then he added: I have the original of this certificate with me in Rome, and it is written all in the hand of the above-mentioned Lord Cardinal Bellarmine.

Q: Whether, when he was notified of the above-mentioned matters, there were others present, and who they were.

A: When Lord Cardinal Bellarmine notified me of what I mentioned regarding Copernicus's opinion, there were some Dominican Fathers present, but I did not know them nor have I seen them since.

Q: Whether at that time, in the presence of those Fathers, he was given any injunction either by them or by someone else concerning the same matter, and if so what.

A: As I remember it, the affair took place in the following manner. One morning Lord Cardinal Bellarmine sent for me, and he told me a certain detail that I should like to speak to the ear of His Holiness before telling others; but then at the end he told me that Copernicus's opinion could not be held [340] or defended, being contrary to Holy Scripture. I do not recall whether those Dominican Fathers were there at first or came afterwards; nor do I recall whether they were present when the Lord Cardinal told me that the said opinion could not be held. Finally, it may be that I was given an injunction not to hold or defend the said opinion, but I do not recall it since this is something of many years ago.

Q: Whether, if one were to read to him what he was then told and ordered with injunction, he would remember that.

A: I do not recall that I was told anything else, nor can I know whether I shall remember what was then told me, even if it is read to me. I am saying freely what I recall because I do not claim not [*sic*][4] to have in any way violated that injunction, that is, not to have held or defended at all the said opinion of the earth's motion and sun's stability.

And having been told that the said injunction, given to him then in the presence of witnesses, states that he cannot in any way hold, defend, or teach

---

4. The original sentence does explicitly have this double negative, suggesting an admission of some wrongdoing on Galileo's part; this is puzzling in view of the denial later on the same page; thus, the double negative may have been a slip of the tongue.

the said opinion, he was asked whether he remembers how and by whom he was so ordered.

A: I do not recall that this injunction was given me any other way than orally by Lord Cardinal Bellarmine. I do remember that the injunction was that I could not hold or defend, and maybe even that I could *not teach*. I do not recall, further, that there was the phrase *in any way whatever*, but maybe there was; in fact, I did not think about it or keep it in mind, having received a few months thereafter Lord Cardinal Bellarmine's certificate dated 26 May, which I have presented and in which is explained the order given to me not to hold or defend the said opinion. Regarding the other two phrases in the said injunction now mentioned, namely *not to teach* and *in any way whatever*, I did not retain them in my memory, I think because they are not contained in the said certificate, which I relied upon and kept as a reminder.

Q: Whether, after the issuing of the said injunction, he obtained any permission to write the book identified by himself, which he later sent to the printer.

A: After the above-mentioned injunction I did not seek permission to write the above-mentioned book which I have identified, because I do not think that by writing this book I was contradicting at all the injunction given me not to hold, defend, or teach the said opinion, but rather that I was refuting it.

Q: Whether he obtained permission for the printing of the same book, by whom, and whether for himself or for someone else.

A: To obtain permission to print the above-mentioned book, although I was receiving profitable offers from France, Germany, and Venice, I refused them and spontaneously came to Rome three years ago to place it into the hands of the chief censor, namely the Master of the Sacred Palace, [341] giving him absolute authority to add, delete, and change as he saw fit. After having it examined very diligently by his associate Father Visconti, the said Master of the Sacred Palace reviewed it again himself and licensed it; that is, having approved the book, he gave me permission but ordered to have the book printed in Rome. Since, in view of the approaching summer, I wanted to go back home to avoid the danger of getting sick, having been away all of May and June, we agreed that I was to return here the autumn immediately following. While I was in Florence, the plague broke out and commerce was stopped; so, seeing that I could not come to Rome, by correspondence I requested of the same Master of the Sacred Palace permission for the book be printed in Florence. He communicated to me that he would want to review my original manuscript, and that therefore I should send it to him. Despite having used every possible care and having contacted even the highest secretaries of the Grand Duke and the directors of the postal service, to try to send the said original safely, I received no assurance that this could be done, and it certainly would have been damaged, washed out, or burned, such was the strictness at the borders. I related to the same Father Master this difficulty concerning the shipping of the book, and he ordered me to have the book again very scrupulously reviewed by a person acceptable to him; the person he was pleased to designate was Father Master Giacinto Stefani, a Dominican, professor of Sacred Scripture at the University of Florence, preacher for the Most Serene Highnesses, and consultant to the Holy Office. The book was handed over by me to the Father Inquisitor of Florence and by the Father Inquisitor to the above-mentioned Father Giacinto Stefani; the latter returned it to the Father Inquisitor, who sent it to Mr. Niccolò dell'Antella, reviewer of books to be printed for the Most Serene Highness of Florence; the printer, named Landini, received it from this Mr. Niccolò and, having negotiated with the Father Inquisitor, printed it, observing strictly every order given by the Father Master of the Sacred Palace.

Q: Whether, when he asked the above-mentioned Master of the Sacred Palace for permission to print the above-mentioned book, he revealed to the same Most Reverend Father Master the injunction previously given to him concerning the directive of the Holy Congregation, mentioned above.

A: When I asked him for permission to print the book, I did not say anything to the Father Master of the Sacred Palace about the above-mentioned injunction because I did not judge it necessary to tell it to him, having no scruples since with the said book I had neither held nor defended the opinion of the earth's motion and sun's stability; on the contrary, in the said book I show the contrary of Copernicus's opinion, and that Copernicus's reasons are invalid and inconclusive.

With this the deposition ended, and he was assigned a certain room in the dormitory of the officials, located in the Palace of the Holy Office, in lieu of prison,[5] with [342] the injunction not to leave it without special permission, under penalty to be decided by the Holy Congregation; and he was ordered to sign below and was sworn to silence.

I, Galileo Galilei have testified as above.

§21. Maculano to Francesco Barberini (28 April 1633)[6]

Yesterday, in accordance with the orders of His Holiness, I reported on Galileo's case to the Most Eminent Lords of the Holy Congregation by

5. From 12 to 30 April 1633, Galileo was detained at the Inquisition palace but allowed to lodge in the prosecutor's apartment; for details, cf. Finocchiaro 2009.
6. Reprinted from Finocchiaro 1989, 276–77; cf. Galilei 1890–1909, 15: 106–7 (no. 2486).

briefly relating its current state. Their Lordships approved what has been done so far, and then they considered various difficulties in regard to the manner of continuing the case and of leading it to a conclusion; for in his deposition Galileo denied what can be clearly seen in the book he wrote, so that if he were to continue in his negative stance it would become necessary to use greater rigor in the administration of justice and less regard for all the ramifications of this business. Finally I proposed a plan, namely that the Holy Congregation grant me the authority to deal extra-judicially with Galileo, in order to make him understand his error and, once having recognized it, to bring him to confess it. The proposal seemed at first too bold, and there did not seem to be much hope of accomplishing this goal as long as one followed the road of trying to convince him with reasons; however, after I mentioned the basis on which I proposed this, they gave me the authority. In order not to lose time, yesterday afternoon I had a discussion with Galileo, and, after exchanging innumerable arguments and answers, by the grace of the Lord I accomplished my purpose: I made him grasp his error, so that he clearly recognized that he had erred and gone too far in his book; he expressed everything with heartfelt words, as if he were relieved by the knowledge of his error; and he was ready for a judicial confession. However, he asked me for a little time to think about the way to render his confession honest, for in regard to the substance he will hopefully proceed as mentioned above.

I have not communicated this to anyone else, but I felt obliged to inform Your Eminence immediately, for I hope His Holiness and Your Eminence will be satisfied that in this manner [107] the case is brought to such a point that it may be settled without difficulty. The Tribunal will maintain its reputation; the culprit can be treated with benignity; and, whatever the final outcome, he will know the favor done to him, with all the consequent satisfactions one wants in this. I am thinking of examining him today to obtain the said confession; after obtaining it, as I hope, the only thing left for me will be to question him about his intention and allow him to present a defense. With this done, he could be granted imprisonment in his own house, as Your Eminence mentioned. And to you I now express my humblest reverence.

§22. Galileo's Second Deposition (30 April 1633)[7]

Called personally to the hall of the Congregations, in the presence and with the assistance of those mentioned above and of myself, the above-mentioned

---

7. Reprinted from Finocchiaro 1989, 277–79; cf. Galilei 1890–1909, 19: 342–44.

Galileo Galilei, who has since then petitioned to be heard, having sworn an oath to tell the truth, was asked by the Fathers the following:

Q: That he state whatever he wished to say.

A: For several days I have been thinking continuously and directly about the interrogations I underwent on the 16th of this month,[8] and in particular about the question whether sixteen years ago I had been prohibited, by order of the Holy Office, from holding, defending, and teaching in any way whatever the opinion, then condemned, of the earth's motion and sun's stability. It dawned on me to reread my printed *Dialogue*, [343] which over the last three years I had not even looked at. I wanted to check very carefully whether, against my purest intention, through my oversight, there might have fallen from my pen not only something enabling readers or superiors to infer a defect of disobedience on my part, but also other details through which one might think of me as a transgressor of the orders of Holy Church. Being at liberty, through the generous approval of superiors, to send one of my servants for errands, I managed to get a copy of my book, and I started to read it with the greatest concentration and to examine it in the most detailed manner. Not having seen it for so long, I found it almost a new book by another author. Now, I freely confess that it appeared to me in several places to be written in such a way that a reader, not aware of my intention, would have had reason to form the opinion that the arguments for the false side, which I intended to confute, were so stated as to be capable of convincing because of their strength, rather than being easy to answer. In particular, two arguments, one based on sunspots and the other on the tides, are presented favorably to the reader as being strong and powerful, more than would seem proper for someone who deemed them to be inconclusive and wanted to confute them, as indeed I inwardly and truly did and do hold them to be inconclusive and refutable. As an excuse for myself, within myself, for having fallen into an error so foreign to my intention, I was not completely satisfied with saying that when one presents arguments for the opposite side with the intention of confuting them, they must be explained in the fairest way and not be made out of straw to the disadvantage of the opponent,[9] especially when one is writing in dialogue form. Being dissatisfied with this excuse, as I said, I resorted to that of the natural gratification everyone feels for his own subtleties and for showing himself to be cleverer than the average man, by finding ingenious and apparent considerations of probability even in favor of false propositions. Nevertheless—even though, to use Cicero's words, "I am more desirous of glory than is suitable"—if I had to write out the same arguments

---

8. The only previous deposition of which we have a record is the one dated 12 April (§20).
9. Here Galileo formulates an extremely important principle, concerning which see Finocchiaro (2010, xli, 132–34; 2011; 2014, 262–64, 316–17).

now, there is no doubt that I would weaken them in such a way that they could not appear to exhibit a force which they really and essentially lack. My error then was, and I confess it, one of vain ambition, pure ignorance, and inadvertence. This is as much as I need to say on this occasion, and it occurred to me as I reread my book.

With this, having obtained his signature, and having sworn him to silence, the Fathers formally concluded the hearing.

I, Galileo Galilei have testified as above.

[344] And returning after a little, he said:

And for greater confirmation that I neither did hold nor do hold as true the condemned opinion of the earth's motion and sun's stability, if, as I desire, I am granted the possibility and the time to prove it more clearly, I am ready to do so. The occasion for it is readily available since in the book already published the speakers agree that after a certain time they should meet again to discuss various physical problems other than the subject already dealt with. Hence, with this pretext to add one or two other Days, I promise to reconsider the arguments already presented in favor of the said false and condemned opinion and to confute them in the most effective way that the blessed God will enable me. So I beg this Holy Tribunal to cooperate with me in this good resolution, by granting me the permission to put it into practice.

And again he signed.

I, Galileo Galilei, affirm the above.

§23. Galileo's Third Deposition (10 May 1633)[10]

Summoned, there appeared personally at the hall of Congregations of the palace of the Holy Office in Rome, in the presence of the very Reverend Father Fra Vincenzo Maculano, O.P., Commissary General of the Holy Office, etc.

Galileo Galilei mentioned above; and, called before his Paternity, the same Father Commissary gave him a deadline of eight days to present his defense, if he wanted and intended to do it.

Having heard this, he said: I understand what Your Paternity has told me. In reply I say that I do want to present something in my defense, namely in order to show the sincerity and purity of my intention, not at all to excuse my having transgressed in some ways, as I have already said. I present the following statement, together with a certificate by the late Most Eminent Lord Cardinal Bellarmine, written with his own hand by the Lord Cardinal himself, of which I earlier presented a copy by my hand. For the rest I rely in every way on the usual mercy and clemency of this Tribunal.

---

10. Reprinted from Finocchiaro 1989, 279; cf. Galilei 1890–1909, 19: 133–34.

After signing his name, he was sent back to the house of the above-mentioned ambassador of the Most Serene Grand Duke, under the conditions already communicated to him.

I, Galileo Galilei, with my own hand.

§24. Galileo's Defense (10 May 1633)[11]

In an earlier interrogation, I was asked whether I had informed the Most Reverend Father Master of the Sacred Palace about the private injunction issued to me sixteen years ago by order of the Holy Office—"not to hold, defend, or teach in any way" the opinion of the earth's motion and sun's stability—and I answered No. Since I was not asked the reason why I did not inform him, I did not have the opportunity to say anything else. Now it seems to me necessary to mention it, in order to reveal my very pure mind, always averse to using simulation and deceit in any of my actions.

[346] I say, then, that at that time some of my enemies were spreading the rumor that I had been called by the Lord Cardinal Bellarmine in order to abjure some opinions and doctrines of mine, that I had had to abjure, that I had also received punishments for them, etc., and so I was forced to resort to His Eminence and to beg him to give me a certificate explaining why I had been called. I received this certificate, written by his own hand, and it is what I attach to the present statement. In it one clearly sees that I was only told not to hold or defend Copernicus's doctrine of the earth's motion and sun's stability; but one cannot see any trace that, besides this general pronouncement applicable to all, I was given any other special order. Having the reminder of this authentic certificate, handwritten by the one who issued the order himself, I did not try to recall or give any other thought to the words used to give me orally the said injunction, to the effect that one cannot defend or hold, etc.; thus, the two phrases besides "holding" and "defending" which I hear are contained in the injunction given to me and recorded, that is, "teaching" and "in any way whatever," struck me as very new and unheard. I do not think I should be mistrusted about the fact that in the course of fourteen or sixteen years I lost any memory of them, especially since I had no need to give the matter any thought, having such a valid reminder in writing. Now, when those two phrases are removed and we retain only the other two mentioned in the attached certificate, there is no reason to doubt that the order contained in it is the same as the injunction issued by the decree of the Holy Congregation of the Index. From this I feel very reasonably excused for not notifying the Father Master of the Sacred Palace of the injunction given to me in private, the latter being the same as the one of the Congregation of the Index.

---

11. Reprinted from Finocchiaro 1989, 279–81; cf. Galilei 1890–1909, 19: 345–47.

Given that my book was not subject to more stringent censures than those required by the decree of the Index, I followed the surest and most effective way to protect it and to purge it of any trace of blemish. It seems to me that this is very obvious, since I handed it over to the supreme Inquisitor [347] at a time when many books on the same subjects were being prohibited solely on account of the above-mentioned decree.

From the things I am saying, I think I can firmly hope that the idea of my having knowingly and willingly disobeyed the orders given me will be kept out of the minds of the Most Eminent and Most Prudent Lord judges. Thus, those flaws that can be seen scattered in my book were not introduced through the cunning of a disguised and insincere intention, but rather through the vain ambition and satisfaction of appearing clever above and beyond the average among popular writers; this was an inadvertent result of my writing, as I confessed in another deposition of mine. I am ready to make amends and to compensate for this flaw by every possible means, whenever I may be either ordered or allowed by their Most Eminent Lordships.

Finally, I am left with asking you to consider the pitiable state of ill health to which I am reduced, due to ten months of constant mental distress, and to the discomforts of a long and tiresome journey in the most awful season and at the age of seventy; I feel I have lost the greater part of the years which my previous state of health promised me. I am encouraged to do this by the faith I have in the clemency and kindness of heart of the Most Eminent Lordships, my judges; and I hope that, if their sense of justice perceives anything lacking among so many ailments as adequate punishment for my crimes, they will, begged by me, condone it out of regard for my declining old age, which I humbly also ask them to consider. Equally, I want them to consider my honor and reputation against the slanders of those who hate me, and I hope that when the latter insist on disparaging my reputation, the Most Eminent Lordships will take it as evidence why it became necessary for me to obtain from the Most Eminent Lord Cardinal Bellarmine the certificate attached herewith.

§25. Inquisition Minutes (16 June 1633)[12]

[282] The meeting of the Holy Office was held at the apostolic palace on the Quirinale hill, in the presence of His Holiness Urban VIII, pope by divine providence; of the most eminent and reverend Lord Cardinals Bentivoglio, di Cremona, Sant'Onofrio, Gessi, Verospi, Ginetti, [283] general inquisitors; and of the Reverend Lord Fathers the Commissary General and the Assessor of the Holy Office. Regarding the cases mentioned below, which the Lord

---

12. Reprinted from Finocchiaro 2005, 247; cf. Galilei 1890–1909, 19: 282–83.

Assessor presented in writing and conveyed to me, the Notary, to wit: . . . For the case of the Florentine Galileo Galilei, detained in this Holy Office and (because of old age and ill health) freed with the injunction not to leave the house where he has chosen to reside in Rome and to appear here whenever requested (on pain of some penalty to be determined by the Sacred Congregation); after the issues were presented, the proceedings were related, etc., and the various opinions were heard; His Holiness decided that the same Galileo is to be interrogated even with the threat of torture;[13] and that if he holds up, after a vehement abjuration at a plenary meeting of the Holy Office, he is to be condemned to prison at the pleasure of the Sacred Congregation, and he is to be enjoined that in the future he must no longer treat in any way (in writing or orally) of the earth's motion or sun's stability, nor of the opposite, on pain of relapse; and that the book written by him and entitled *Dialogue of Galileo Galilei Lincean* is to be prohibited. Moreover, so that these things be known to all, he ordered that copies of the sentence containing the above be transmitted to all apostolic nuncios and to all inquisitors for heretical depravity, and especially to the inquisitor of Florence, who is to publicly read that sentence at a plenary meeting to which must be personally summoned the greatest possible number of professors of the mathematical sciences.

§26. Galileo's Fourth Deposition (21 June 1633)[14]

Called personally to the hall of Congregations in the palace of the Holy Office in Rome, fully in the presence of the Reverend Father Commissary General of the Holy Office, assisted by the Reverend Father Prosecutor, etc.

Galileo Galilei, Florentine, mentioned previously, having sworn an oath to tell the truth, was asked by the Fathers the following:

Q: Whether he had anything to say.

A: I have nothing to say.

Q: Whether he holds or has held, and for how long, that the sun is the center of the world and the earth is not the center of the world but moves also with diurnal motion.

A: A long time ago, that is, before the decision of the Holy Congregation of the Index, and before I was issued that injunction, I was undecided and regarded the two opinions, those of Ptolemy and Copernicus, as disputable, because either the one or the other could be true in nature. But after the above-mentioned decision, assured by the prudence of the authorities, all my uncertainty stopped, and I held, as I still hold, as very true

---

13. On the issue of torture, cf. §26 and see Finocchiaro 2009.
14. Reprinted from Finocchiaro 1989, 286–87; cf. Galilei 1890–1909, 19: 361–62.

and undoubted Ptolemy's opinion, namely the stability of the earth and the motion of the sun.

Having been told that he is presumed to have held the said opinion after that time, from the manner and procedure in which the said opinion is discussed and defended in the book he published after that time, indeed from the very fact that he wrote and published the said book, therefore he was asked to freely tell the truth whether he holds or has held that opinion.

A: In regard to my writing of the *Dialogue* already published, I did not do so because I held Copernicus's opinion to be true. Instead, deeming only to be doing a beneficial service, I explained the physical and astronomical reasons that can be advanced for one side and for the other; I tried to show that none of these, neither those in favor of this opinion or that, had the strength of a conclusive proof and that therefore to proceed with certainty one had to resort to the determination of more subtle doctrines, as one can see in many places in the *Dialogue*. So for my part I conclude [362] that I do not hold and, after the determination of the authorities, I have not held the condemned opinion.

Having been told that from the book itself and the reasons advanced for the affirmative side, namely that the earth moves and the sun is motionless, he is presumed, as it was stated, that he holds Copernicus's opinion, or at least that he held it at the time, therefore he was told that unless he decided to proffer the truth, one would have recourse to the remedies of the law and to appropriate steps against him.

A: I do not hold this opinion of Copernicus, and I have not held it after being ordered by injunction to abandon it. For the rest, here I am in your hands; do as you please.

And he was told to tell the truth, otherwise one would have recourse to torture.[15]

A: I am here to obey, but I have not held this opinion after the determination was made, as I said.

And since nothing else could be done for the execution of the decision,[16] after he signed he was sent to his place.

I, Galileo Galilei, have testified as above.

§27. Inquisition's Sentence (22 June 1633)[17]

We: Gaspare Borgia, with the title of the Holy Cross in Jerusalem; Fra Felice Centini, with the title of Santa Anastasia, called d'Ascoli; Guido Bentivoglio,

---

15. Again, on torture, cf. §25 and see Finocchiaro 2009.
16. That is, the pope's decision at the Inquisition meeting of 16 June (§25).
17. Reprinted from Finocchiaro 1989, 287–91; cf. Galilei 1890–1909, 19: 402–6.

with the title of Santa Maria del Popolo; Fra Desiderio Scaglia, with the title of San Carlo, called di Cremona; Fra Antonio Barberini, called di Sant'Onofrio; Laudivio Zacchia, with the title of San Pietro in Vincoli, called di San Sisto; [403] Berlinghiero Gessi, with the title of Sant'Agostino; Fabrizio Verospi, with the title of San Lorenzo in Panisperna, of the order of priests; Francesco Barberini, with the title of San Lorenzo in Damaso; and Marzio Ginetti, with the title of Santa Maria Nuova, of the order of deacons;

By the grace of God, Cardinals of the Holy Roman Church, and especially commissioned by the Holy Apostolic See as Inquisitors-General against heretical depravity in all of Christendom.

Whereas you, Galileo, son of the late Vincenzio Galilei, Florentine, aged seventy years, were denounced to this Holy Office in 1615 for holding as true the false doctrine taught by some that the sun is the center of the world and motionless and the earth moves even with diurnal motion; for having disciples to whom you taught the same doctrine; for being in correspondence with some German mathematicians about it; for having published some letters entitled *On Sunspots*, in which you explained the same doctrine as true; for interpreting Holy Scripture according to your own meaning in response to objections based on Scripture which were sometimes made to you; and whereas later we received a copy of an essay in the form of a letter, which was said to have been written by you to a former disciple of yours, and which in accordance with Copernicus's position contains various propositions against the authority and true meaning of the Holy Scripture;

And whereas this Holy Tribunal wanted to remedy the disorder and the harm which derived from it and which was growing to the detriment of the Holy Faith, by order of His Holiness and the Most Eminent and Most Reverend Lord Cardinals of this Supreme and Universal Inquisition, the Consultant Theologians assessed the two propositions of the sun's stability and the earth's motion as follows:

That the sun is the center of the world and motionless is a proposition which is philosophically absurd and false, and formally heretical, for being explicitly contrary to Holy Scripture;

That the earth is neither the center of the world nor motionless but moves even with diurnal motion is philosophically equally absurd and false, and theologically at least erroneous in the Faith.

Whereas however we wanted to treat you with benignity at that time, it was decided at the Holy Congregation held in the presence of His Holiness on 25 February 1616 that the Most Eminent Lord Cardinal Bellarmine would order you to abandon this false opinion completely; that if you refused to do this, the Commissary of the Holy Office would give you an injunction to abandon this doctrine, not to teach it to others, not to defend it, and not to treat of it; and that if you did not acquiesce in this injunction, you should be imprisoned. To execute this decision, the following day at the palace of and in the presence of the above-mentioned Most Eminent Lord Cardinal Bellarmine, after being informed and warned in a friendly way by the same Lord Cardinal, you were given an injunction by the then Father Commissary of the Holy Office [404] in the presence of a notary and witnesses to the effect that you must completely abandon the said false opinion, and that in the future you could neither hold, nor defend, nor teach it in any way whatever, either orally or in writing; having promised to obey, you were dismissed.

Furthermore, in order to do away completely with such a pernicious doctrine, and not let it creep any longer to the great detriment of Catholic truth, the Holy Congregation of the Index issued a decree which prohibited books treating of such a doctrine, and which declared it false and wholly contrary to the divine and Holy Scripture.

And whereas a book has appeared here lately, printed in Florence last year, whose inscription showed that you were the author, the title being *Dialogue by Galileo Galilei on the Two Chief World Systems, Ptolemaic and Copernican*; and whereas the Holy Congregation was informed that with the printing of this book the false opinion of the earth's motion and sun's stability was being disseminated and taking hold more and more every day, the said book was diligently examined and was found to violate explicitly the above-mentioned injunction given to you; for in the same book you have defended the said opinion already condemned and so declared to your face, although in the said book you try by means of various subterfuges to give the impression of leaving it undecided and labeled as probable; this is still a very serious error since there is no way an opinion declared and defined contrary to divine Scripture may be probable.

Therefore, by our order you were summoned to this Holy Office, where, examined under oath, you acknowledged the book as written and published by you. You confessed that about ten or twelve years ago, after having been given the injunction mentioned above, you began writing the said book, and that you asked for permission to print it without explaining to those who gave you such permission that you were under the injunction of not holding, defending, or teaching such a doctrine in any way whatever.

Likewise, you confessed that in several places the exposition of the said book is expressed in such a way that a reader could get the idea that the arguments given for the false side were effective enough to be capable of convincing, rather than being easy to refute. Your excuses for having committed an error, as you said so foreign from your intention, were that you had written in dialogue form, and that everyone feels a natural satisfaction for one's own subtleties and for showing oneself sharper than the average man by finding ingenious and apparently probable arguments even in favor of false propositions.

Having been given suitable terms to present your defense, you produced a certificate in the handwriting of the Most Eminent Lord Cardinal Bellarmine, which you said you obtained to defend yourself from the calumnies of your enemies, who were claiming that you had abjured and had been punished by the Holy Office. This [405] certificate says that you had neither abjured nor been punished, but only that you had been notified of the declaration made by His Holiness and published by the Holy Congregation of the Index, whose content is that the doctrine of the earth's motion and sun's stability is contrary to Holy Scripture and so can be neither defended nor held. Because this certificate does not contain the two phrases of the injunction, namely "to teach" and "in any way whatever," one is supposed to believe that in the course of fourteen or sixteen years you had lost any recollection of them, and that for this same reason you had been silent about the injunction when you applied for the license to publish the book. Furthermore, one is supposed to believe that you point out all of this not to excuse the error, but in order to have it attributed to conceited ambition rather than to malice. However, the said certificate you produced in your defense aggravates your case further since, while it says that the said opinion is contrary to Holy Scripture, yet you dared to treat of it, defend it, and show it as probable; nor are you helped by the license you artfully and cunningly extorted, since you did not mention the injunction you were under.

Because we did not think you had said the whole truth about your intention, we deemed it necessary to proceed against you by a rigorous examination. Here you answered in a Catholic manner, though without prejudice to the above-mentioned things confessed by you and deduced against you about your intention.

Therefore, having seen and seriously considered the merits of your case, together with the above-mentioned confessions and excuses and with any other reasonable matter worth seeing and considering, we have come to the final sentence against you given below.

Therefore, invoking the Most Holy name of Our Lord Jesus Christ and of his most glorious Mother, ever Virgin Mary; and sitting as a tribunal, with the advice and counsel of the Reverend Masters of Sacred Theology and the Doctors of both laws, our consultants; in this written opinion we pronounce final judgment on the case pending before us between the Magnificent Carlo Sinceri, Doctor of both laws and Prosecuting Attorney of this Holy Office, on one side, and you the above-mentioned Galileo Galilei, the culprit here present, examined, tried, and confessed as above, on the other side:

We say, pronounce, sentence, and declare that you, the above-mentioned Galileo, because of the things deduced in the trial and confessed by you as above, have rendered yourself according to this Holy Office vehemently sus-pected of heresy,[18] namely of having held and believed a doctrine which is false and contrary to the divine and Holy Scripture: that the sun is the center of the world and does not move from east to west, and the earth moves and is not the center of the world, and that one may hold and defend as probable an opinion after it has been declared and defined contrary to Holy Scripture. Consequently you have incurred all the censures and penalties imposed and promulgated by the sacred canons and all particular and general laws against such delinquents. We are willing to absolve you from them provided that first, with a sincere heart and unfeigned faith, in front of us you abjure, curse, and detest the above-mentioned errors and [406] heresies, and every other error and heresy contrary to the Catholic and Apostolic Church, in the manner and form we will prescribe to you.

Furthermore, so that this serious and pernicious error and transgression of yours does not remain completely unpunished, and so that you will be more cautious in the future and an example for others to abstain from similar crimes, we order that the book *Dialogue* by Galileo Galilei be prohibited by public edict.

We condemn you to formal imprisonment in this Holy Office at our plea-sure. As a salutary penance we impose on you to recite the seven penitential psalms once a week for the next three years. And we reserve the authority to moderate, change, or condone wholly or in part the above-mentioned penal-ties and penances.

This we say, pronounce, sentence, declare, order, and reserve by this or any other better manner or form that we reasonably can or shall think of.

So we the undersigned[19] Cardinals pronounce: Felice Cardinal d'Ascoli; Guido Cardinal Bentivoglio; Fra Desiderio Cardinal di Cremona; Fra Antonio Cardinal di Sant'Onofrio; Berlinghiero Cardinal Gessi; Fabrizio Cardinal Verospi; Marzio Cardinal Ginetti.

§28. Galileo's Abjuration (22 June 1633)[20]

I, Galileo, son of the late Vincenzio Galilei of Florence, seventy years of age, arraigned personally for judgment, kneeling before you Most Eminent and Most Reverend Cardinals Inquisitors-General against heretical depravity in all

---

18. As discussed in the Introduction (§0.2), "vehement suspicion of heresy" was a technical term meaning a specific category of religious crime, intermediate in serious-ness between "formal heresy" and "slight suspicion of heresy."
19. Note that only seven out of the ten cardinals in the Congregation signed the sentence.
20. Reprinted from Finocchiaro 1989, 292–93; cf. Galilei 1890–1909, 19: 406–7.

of Christendom, having before my eyes and touching with my hands the Holy Gospels, swear that I have always believed, I believe now, and with God's help I will believe in the future all that the Holy Catholic and Apostolic Church holds, preaches, and teaches. However, whereas, after having been judicially instructed with injunction by the Holy Office to abandon completely the false opinion that the sun is the center of the world and does not move and the earth is not the center of the world and moves, and not to hold, defend, or teach this false doctrine in any way whatever, orally or in writing; and after having been notified that this doctrine is contrary to Holy Scripture; I wrote and published a book in which I treat of this already condemned doctrine and adduce very effective reasons in its favor, without refuting them in any way; therefore, I have been judged vehemently suspected of heresy, namely of having held and believed that the sun is the center of the world and motionless and the earth is not the center and moves.

Therefore, desiring to remove from the minds of Your Eminences and every faithful [407] Christian this vehement suspicion, rightly conceived against me, with a sincere heart and unfeigned faith I abjure, curse, and detest the above-mentioned errors and heresies, and in general each and every other error, heresy, and sect contrary to the Holy Church; and I swear that in the future I will never again say or assert, orally or in writing, anything which might cause a similar suspicion about me; on the contrary, if I should come to know any heretic or anyone suspected of heresy, I will denounce him to this Holy Office, or to the Inquisitor or Ordinary of the place where I happen to be.

Furthermore, I swear and promise to comply with and observe completely all the penances which have been or will be imposed upon me by this Holy Office; and should I fail to keep any of these promises and oaths, which God forbid, I submit myself to all the penalties and punishments imposed and promulgated by the sacred canons and other particular and general laws against similar delinquents. So help me God and these Holy Gospels of His, which I touch with my hands.

I, the above-mentioned Galileo Galilei, have abjured, sworn, promised, and obliged myself as above; and in witness of the truth I have signed with my own hand the present document of abjuration and have recited it word for word in Rome, at the convent of the Minerva, this twenty-second day of June 1633.

I, Galileo Galilei, have abjured as above, by my own hand.

CHAPTER 6

Reports and Responses: Implementation of Sentence

§29. Orders to Nuncios and Inquisitors (2 July 1633)[1]

The Congregation of the Index had suspended Nicolaus Copernicus's treatise *On the Revolutions of the Heavenly Spheres* because that book maintains that the earth moves, and not the sun, which is the center of the world, an opinion contrary to Sacred Scripture; and several years ago this Sacred Congregation of the Holy Office had prohibited Galileo Galilei of Florence from holding, defending, or teaching in any way whatever, orally or in writing, the said opinion. Nevertheless, the same Galileo has dared to write a book titled *[Dialogo di] Galileo Galilei Linceo;* without revealing the said prohibition, he has extorted the permission to print it and has had it printed; claiming at the beginning, within the body, and at the end of that book to want to treat hypothetically of the said opinion of Copernicus (although he could not treat of it in any manner), he has however treated of it in such a way that he became vehemently suspected of having held such an opinion. Thus, he was tried and detained in this Holy Office, and the sentence of these Most Eminent Lords condemned him to abjure the said opinion, to stay under formal arrest subject to the wishes of their Eminences, and to do other salutary penances. Your Reverence can see all that in the attached copy of the sentence and abjuration; this document is sent to you so that you can transmit it to your vicars and it can be known by them and by all professors of philosophy and of mathematics; for, knowing how the said Galileo has been treated, they can understand the seriousness of the error he committed, and avoid it together with the punishment they would receive if they were to fall into it. By way of ending, may God the Lord preserve you.

---

1. Reprinted from Finocchiaro 2005, 27; cf. Galilei 1890–1909, 15: 169 (no. 2566). This memorandum was signed by Antonio Barberini; for more details, see Finocchiaro 2005, 26–28.

§30. Buonamici's Account (July 1633)[2]

[407] Galileo Galilei, a Florentine, professor of philosophy and mathematics, nicknamed professor of the spyglass[3] or telescope, is too well known to the world for me to have to give an account of his personal life on the occasion of relating the long molestation he suffered because of the system of Nicolaus Copernicus. Many decades ago, the latter wrote a book on the constitution of the universe in which he contradicted Aristotle and Ptolemy; he asserted it is not true that, as they say, the earth is motionless, nor that it is the center of the world, nor that the immense structures of the planets and the heavens turn around this miniscule terrestrial globe in the period of twenty-four hours by being carried by the imagined sphere of the Prime Mobile. [408] Instead he said that the sun is the center of the world and motionless in regard to displacement, but moving by rotation on itself; that the planets we see moving in the heavens revolve around it according to their periods; that the earth does the same by an annual motion in the plane of the ecliptic, being located between Venus and Mars; and that it also rotates on itself by a diurnal motion from west to east, which allows it to see in twenty-four hours all the heavens, stars, and planets. Few have believed or noticed this opinion of Copernicus on account of both its extravagance and the implausibilities involving human sense-experience which it seems to imply. However, the sensible demonstration of the new spyglass or telescope seemed to flatten many difficulties and implausibilities which natural vision cannot grasp; thus, many thinkers, and especially the said Galileo, argued that the system of Copernicus deserved better consideration than had been the case in the past; at the same time, they greatly admired his mind because, without having the convenience of the telescope, he still was able to understand some properties and features of the planets that strengthened his opinion and cannot be discerned by the natural eye without using the telescope; for example, when Venus and Mars are nearer the earth they are seen, respectively, forty and sixty times larger than when they are farther and appear smaller; and when Venus is near conjunction with the sun, it appears sickle-shaped, as the moon does when it is new.

These and other sensible demonstrations, which Galileo with the benefit of the telescope discovered in the heavens before anyone else, excited envy in many persons; being envious for his glory and unable to contradict the manifest

---

2. Reprinted from Finocchiaro 2005, 33–36; cf. Galilei 1890–1909, 19: 407–11. In 1633, Buonamici happened to be living in Rome, and so it is likely that he learned about the trial firsthand; he sent copies of his account to Galileo and to several persons in Germany, Spain, and Flanders; for more details, see Finocchiaro 2005, 33, 36.

3. *Spyglass* was the term used by Galileo to refer to the telescope during the first two years that he used the instrument (*perspicillum* in Latin, *occhiale* in Italian); in 1611 the term *telescopium* was coined, and he adopted the new term.

truth of the discoveries made in the heavens, they started to persecute him; this was especially true for some Dominican friars who took the road of the Inquisition and Holy Office in Rome, complaining that he attributed stability to the sun and mobility to the earth against the words of Sacred Scripture. Thus, Paul V, instigated by the same friars, would have declared this Copernican system erroneous and heretical, insofar as it is contrary to the teaching of Scripture in various places and especially in Joshua, had it not been for the opposition and defense of Lord Cardinal Maffeo Barberini (today Pope Urban VIII) and of Lord Cardinal Bonifacio Caetani. [409] However, these cardinals argued, first, that Nicolaus Copernicus could not be declared heretical for a purely natural doctrine, without eliciting the laughter of the heretics, who do not accept the reform of the calendar of which he was the principal master. Second, it did not seem prudent to assert on the authority of Sacred Scripture that in purely natural subjects something is true which (with the passage of time and by means of sensible demonstrations) could be discovered to be false; for even in subjects concerning Faith (which is the principal if not only purpose of Sacred Scripture), it is frequently necessary to understand that it speaks in accordance with our abilities; otherwise, if one wanted to abide by the pure sound of the words, one would end up in errors and impieties (such as that God has hands, feet, emotions, etc.). Thus, these cardinals dissuaded Paul V from the ruling that the said friars had come close to extracting from him. These friars have shown themselves to be persecutors more of the person than of the opinion; for after it was asserted by Copernicus, no one persecuted it in the period of so many years, whereas when Galileo merely discussed it they made him appear before the dreadful tribunal of the Holy Office. At that time, the pontifical decree was reduced to ordering that the system of the sun's stability and the earth's mobility could be neither held nor defended because it appeared to be contrary to the account in Sacred Scripture.

Thereafter Galileo, obeying this order, no longer gave any thought to this subject, until the year 1624 when Lord Cardinal Hohenzollern provided the following encouragement: he said that he had spoken with the current pontiff about this opinion; that His Holiness had recalled defending Copernicus at the time of Paul V; and that His Holiness assured him that he would never allow this opinion to be declared heretical, if for no other reason than for the veneration rightly due to the memory of Nicolaus Copernicus.[4] Spurred by this, Galileo started writing a book in the form of a dialogue; in it he examined the foundations and reasons of the two different systems, Aristotelian and Copernican, and without leaning more on one side than on the other, he left the matter undecided. He himself brought this book to Rome in the year 1630 and placed it in the hands of His Holiness, who with his own hand corrected something in

---

4. Cf. Galileo to Cesi, 8 June 1624, in Galilei 1890–1909, 13: 182–83 (no. 1637).

the title; then it was examined by the Master of the Sacred Palace, and returned with his endorsement [410] and with a preface produced and compiled by order of His Holiness, which the printed book indeed carries. Approved in the manner described above, it was printed in Florence.

This awakened once again his old persecutors, who were joined by those who quarreled with them about *de auxiliis*,[5] out of personal spite between someone from their order and Galileo, concerning who was the first to discover sunspots;[6] and so they brought new complaints before the same tribunal, which is always open to accusations and ready to fulminate censures and excommunications against free thought. There was in addition a hatred and persecution (typical of friars) by Father Firenzuola, the Commissary of the Holy Office much loved by His Holiness more for knowing civil engineering and accounting than for preaching or theology, against Father Mostro,[7] Master of the Sacred Palace and approver of the book. The pope was unwilling to prevent Firenzuola from allowing the filing of complaints against Galileo in order to harm Father Mostro and Ciampoli, another friend and supporter of Galileo; and the pope allowed that Galileo be summoned and forced to come to Rome despite the plague in Florence, the harshness of the winter, and the age of sixty years.[8]

Galileo obeyed, against the opinion and advice of his truest friends, who argued that he should move abroad, write an apology, and not expose himself to the impertinent and ambitious passion of a friar. He came to Rome, and they held him for two months at the house of the Tuscan ambassador, without ever telling him anything other than that he should not go out or engage in conversations. Finally, they made him go to the Holy Office; they kept him in free custody for eleven days;[9] and they examined him only about the imprimatur and approval of the book. He said he received it from the Master of the Sacred Palace. Then they sent him back to the house of the same ambassador, with the same order not to go out or socialize.

---

5. The controversy *de auxiliis* was a dispute between Dominicans and Jesuits that raged for decades in the late sixteenth and early seventeenth centuries. It involved subtle theological points about the nature of grace, predestination, free will, personal merit, and eternal salvation. It threatened to split the Church until 1607, when Pope Paul V decreed that for the time being it did not have to be authoritatively resolved, and that in the future neither side can act as if the other were heretical; then in 1611 the Inquisition prohibited all writings on the subject unless they received its own special approval.
6. Christoph Scheiner.
7. *Mostro* (which literally means "monster") was the nickname of Niccolò Riccardi, because of his large size.
8. This number is not exactly right; born in 1564, Galileo was sixty-nine in 1633.
9. Actually eighteen days (12–30 April 1633), during which Galileo was detained at the Inquisition palace but allowed to lodge in the prosecutor's apartment; for details, see Finocchiaro 2009.

Thus they turned the persecution against Father Mostro. He first excused himself by saying that His Holiness himself had ordered him to approve the book; but when the pope denied it and became angry, Father Mostro said that it was secretary Ciampoli who had conveyed to him the order of His Holiness. The pope replied that there was no such order. Finally, Father Mostro produced a note by Ciampoli stating that His Holiness was ordering the book's approval (and was present while Ciampoli was writing). Seeing therefore that Father Mostro could not be successfully attacked, the commissary did not want to seem to have conducted the proceedings in vain, and became more influenced by the strong requests of the old enemies of Galileo and of the new pretenders to the discovery of sunspots.

And so Galileo was made to appear before the Congregation of the Holy Office and to formally abjure the opinion of Copernicus, even though this was superfluous for him, since he had not [411] held or defended it but had only discussed it. Galileo thus saw himself forced to do something he would have never believed, especially because the commissary Father Firenzuola in their conversations had never mentioned such an abjuration. However, he pleaded with the Lord Cardinals that since they were proceeding with him in that manner, they could make him say whatever their Eminences wanted, except only two things: one, that he would not have to say that he was not a Catholic, for such he was and wanted to die, in spite of and out of spite for his detractors; the other, that he also could not say that he had ever deceived anyone, especially in the publication of his book, which he had submitted for ecclesiastical censorship and had had printed with a legitimate approval. After this protestation, he read what Father Firenzuola had written. Later, with the permission of His Holiness, he left toward Tuscany, having learned from experience that perhaps it would have been better to follow the advice of his friends than to obey the angry persecutions of his enemies.

§31. Galileo to Diodati (25 July 1634)[10]

[115] I hope that, after you hear about my past and present troubles together with other suspected future ones, Your Lordship and the other friends and patrons near you will excuse me for my delay in answering your letters and my total silence regarding theirs, as Your Lordship can make them aware of the sinister direction in which my affairs are going at this time.

In my sentence in Rome, I was condemned by the Holy Office to prison at the discretion of His Holiness, who assigned me as prison the grand duke's

10. Reprinted from Finocchiaro 2005, 57–58; cf. Galilei 1890–1909, 16: 115–17, lines 1–71 (no. 2970). For more details, see Finocchiaro 2005, 56–59.

palace and garden at Trinità dei Monti. This happened last year in the month of June, and I was [116] given to understand that after that month and the following one, if I had petitioned for a pardon and total liberation, I would have obtained it; but in order not to have to stay there the whole summer and also part of the autumn (and suffer the restrictions of such a season), I obtained a commutation to Siena, where I was assigned the archbishop's house. I lived there for five months, after which the prison was commuted to the limits of this small villa, a mile away from Florence, with a very strict prohibition against going into the city, holding conversations or meetings of many friends together, or inviting them to banquets.

I was living here very quietly, frequently visiting a nearby monastery where my two daughters were nuns. I loved them very much, especially the elder, a woman of exquisite mind and singular goodness and extremely attached to me.[11] Due to an accumulation of melancholy humors during my absence (which she considered to be troublesome) and to a sudden dysentery acquired later, my elder daughter died within six days at the age of thirty-three and left me in extreme grief.

This was doubled by another unfortunate event. I was returning home from the convent in the company of the physician who had examined my sick daughter just before she passed away, and who was telling me that her condition was quite hopeless and that she would not have lasted more than the following day, as indeed it turned out. When I arrived home I found the inquisitor's deputy, who had come to convey to me an order from the Holy Office in Rome received by the inquisitor in a letter from Lord Cardinal Barberini. I was ordered to stop submitting any more petitions for a pardon and for permission to return to Florence, otherwise they would recall me to Rome and hold me in the real prison of the Holy Office. This was the reply given to the memorandum which, after nine months of exile on my part, the Lord Ambassador of Tuscany had presented to that Tribunal. From this reply, I think one can conjecture that very likely my present prison will not end, except by turning into the one that is universal, most strict, and eternal.

From this and other incidents which it would take too long to write about, one sees that the anger of my very powerful enemies is constantly becoming exacerbated. They finally have chosen to reveal themselves. That is, about two months ago a good friend of mine was [117] in Rome talking to Father Christoph Grienberger, a Jesuit and a mathematician at the College there. When they came to discussing what happened to me, the Jesuit said these

11. Virginia Galilei (1600–1634), who took the name Sister Maria Celeste when she became a nun at age sixteen; in October 1633, upon reading the text of the Inquisition sentence against her father, she assumed the burden of sharing his religious penance of reciting the seven penitential psalms once a week for three years. Cf. Finocchiaro 2005, 51–52; Sobel 1999.

exact words: "If Galileo had been able to retain the affection of the Fathers of this College, he would be living in worldly glory; none of his misfortunes would have happened; and he could have written at will on any subject, I say even of the earth's motions, etc." So Your Lordship sees that it is not this or that opinion which has provoked and provokes the war against me, but to have fallen out of favor with the Jesuits.

I have other indications of the vigilance of my persecutors. One example involves a letter written to me from a transalpine country and sent to me in Rome, where the writer must have thought that I was still residing; it was intercepted and brought to Lord Cardinal Barberini. According to what was later written to me from Rome, fortunately the letter was not a reply but a first contact, and it was full of praises for my *Dialogue*. It was seen by many persons, and I understand that copies are circulating in Rome; and I have been told that I will be able to see it. Add to this other mental troubles and many bodily ailments; at my age over seventy, they keep me depressed in such a way that any small effort is tiring and hard. Thus, for all these reasons my friends must sympathize with me and forgive my failures, which look like negligence but are really impotence; and since Your Lordship more than anyone else is partial toward me, you must help me to maintain the goodwill of those there who are well disposed toward me.

§32. Peiresc's Plea for a Pardon (5 December 1634)[12]

[169] Finally, I have to make a plea to Your Eminence, and I beg you (as much I know how and am capable of) to excuse the daring of this most faithful servant of yours, and to blame on the usual confidence you show me the hope I nurture from the sublime goodness of Your Eminence. [170] My hope is that you will deign yourself to do something for the consolation of a good old septuagenarian, who is in ill health and whose memory will be difficult to erase in the future. He may have erred in regard to some proposition (as human nature allows), but without showing obstinacy of opinion, and instead underwriting the opposite opinion in accordance with the orders received; so please do not keep him in the kind of confinement which I understand is being applied in his case, if it is possible to obtain some relaxation, as the natural kindness of Your Eminence makes me hope. I met him thirty-four or more years ago at the University of Padua and at the most beautiful conversations we enjoyed at the house of Giovanni Vincenzio Pinelli (God bless his soul), together with Messrs. Aleandro and Pignoria (God bless their souls). It

---

12. Reprinted from Finocchiaro 2005, 53–54; cf. Galilei 1890–1909, 16: 215–16 (no. 3026). For more details, see Finocchiaro 2005, 52–56.

will be difficult for posterity not to show him eternal gratitude for the admirable novelties he discovered in the heavens by means of his telescope and his extremely penetrating mind.

Recall that in regard to Tertullian, Origen, and many other Church Fathers who fell into some errors due to simple-mindedness or other reason, the Holy Church (like a good mother) has not failed to show them great veneration on account of their other ideas and other indications of their piety and zeal in the service of God. On the contrary, she would regard as perverse and would reproach the zeal of whoever would want to punish them with the same severity with which obstinate heretics are punished, or administer to them those penalties that can be applied to persons guilty of some great error or crime; such is human weakness, which may have been the source of some of their sins, and their fragility is sometimes worthy of excuse and forgiveness, as has happened in more serious cases involving persons who hold the first places among the saints. Similarly, future centuries may find it strange that, after he retracted an opinion which had not yet been absolutely prohibited in public and which he had proposed merely as a problem, so much rigor should be used against a pitiable old septuagenarian as to keep him in a (private if not public) prison: he is not allowed to return to his city and his house or to receive visits and comfort from friends; he has infirmities that are almost inseparable from old age and require almost continuous assistance; and often this help cannot be subject to the delay due to the distance from the villa to the city, when there is an emergency or an immediate remedy is needed.

I say all this out of compassion for the pitiable good old man Mr. Galileo Galilei, to whom I had wanted to write lately. Thus, having asked the advice of a Florentine friend to know where he could be found, I was told that he was confined to his villa near a monastery, where one of his daughters (his only consolation) was a nun and had recently died, and that he was forbidden to receive visits and correspondence from friends and to go to his city and his house. This shook my heart and drove me to tears, as I considered the vicissitudes of human affairs and the fact that he had had so many uncommon honors and accomplishments, whose memory will last for centuries. I know that painters who excelled in their art have had pardoned extremely serious sins whose enormity was most horrifying, in order not to let their other merit go to waste. So, is it not the case that so many inventions (the most noble that have been discovered in so many centuries) deserve a display of indulgence toward a philosophical play[13] in which he never categorically asserted that his own personal opinion was the one that had been disapproved?

---

13. "Philosophical play" is my rendition of *scherzo problematico*; Peiresc is characterizing the *Dialogue* as a "philosophical play." For the significance of this interpretation, see Finocchiaro 2005, 54–55, 376 n. 48 and n. 53.

[171] This will really be deemed most cruel everywhere, and more by posterity, for it seems that in the present century everyone neglects the interests of the public (especially of the disadvantaged) in order to look after his own. And indeed it will be a stain on the splendor and fame of this Pontificate, if Your Eminence does not decide to take some precaution and some particular care, as I beg and implore you to do most humbly and with the greatest zeal and urgency which I can legitimately display toward you. I also beg you to pardon the liberty I take, which may be too great, but it is important that sometimes your faithful servants be allowed to give you these indications of their faithfulness; for I do not think that the other servants around you would dare to reveal to you in this manner the thoughts which they have in their heart and which touch the honor of Your Eminence much more than it may seem to many.

§33. Galileo to Peiresc (21 February 1635)[14]

[215] I could never by means of a pen express to Your Most Illustrious Lordship the joy given to me by the reading of the most formal and most prudent letter which you wrote on my behalf, and a copy of which was sent me by my relative and patron Mr. Roberto;[15] I received it only yesterday. My pleasure was and is infinite, not because I hope for any improvement, but because I saw a Lord and Patron of such excellent qualities empathize with my condition with such tender affection, and be moved to attempt with such ardent spirit and with such generous as well as moderate daring an undertaking that has rendered silent so many others who are favorably inclined toward my innocence. Oh, if my misfortunes produce for me such sweetness, may my enemies engage in new machinations, for I will always be thankful to them!

I said, my Most Illustrious Lord, that I do not hope for any improvement, and this is so because I did not commit any crime. I could hope to obtain clemency and pardon if I had erred, because mistakes are the subject matter over which princes can exercise the power of reprieve and pardon; but in regard to someone who has been unjustly condemned, it suits them to maintain rigor, as a cover for the legality of the proceedings.

---

14. Reprinted from Finocchiaro 2005, 59–60; cf. Galilei 1890–1909, 16: 215–16 (no. 3082). For more details, see Finocchiaro 2005, 59–61.

15. Roberto Galilei (born in Florence in 1595) was a distant relative of Galileo; he had moved to Lyons and become a French citizen in order to pursue opportunities as a merchant.

And believe me, Your Most Illustrious Lordship, also for your own conso-lation, that this rigor afflicts me less than what others may think, because there are two comforts that constantly assist me. One is that in reading all my works, no one can find the least shadow of anything that deviates from piety and reverence for the Holy Church. The other is my conscience, which is fully known only by me on earth and by God in heaven; it understands perfectly that in the controversy for which I suffer, many people might have been able to proceed and to speak more knowledgeably, but no one (even among the Holy Fathers) could have proceeded and spoken more piously, or with greater zeal toward the Holy Church, or in short with a holier intention than I did. This most religious and most holy [216] intention of mine would appear all the more pure if one were to expose into the open all the calumnies, scams, stratagems, and deceptions that were used in Rome eighteen years ago to cloud the vision of the authorities!

But there is at present no need for me to give you any other greater justifications of my sincerity; for you have been gracious enough to read my writings and may very well have understood what was the true, real, and first motive that under a feigned religious mask has been waging a war against me, constantly laying siege to me and blocking all roads in such a way that neither can help come to me from the outside, nor can I any longer get out to defend myself. In fact, a direct order has gone out to all inquisi-tors not to allow the reprinting of any of my works that have already been published years ago, nor to license any new one which I might want to publish; thus, not only am I supposed to accept and ignore the great many criticisms dealing with purely natural subjects made against me to suppress the doctrine and advertise my ignorance, but also I am supposed to swal-low the sneers, bites, and insults recklessly thrown at me by people more ignorant than I.

But I want to stop making complaints, although I have barely scratched the surface. Nor do I want to keep any longer Your Most Illustrious Lord-ship or bother you with distasteful things; instead I must beg you to excuse me if, drawn by the natural relief which those who suffer get occasionally when they unburden themselves to their most trusted confidants, I have taken too much liberty to annoy you. There remains for me to convey to you with the power of my heart those thanks which I could never convey with words for the humane and compassionate task you undertook on my behalf; you were able to present the case so effectively that, if I do not ben-efit, we can be pretty sure that it must have caused some twinge of remorse in the recipients, who, being men, cannot be devoid of humanity. I con-tinue to be your most obliged and most devout servant. May God the Lord repay the merit of the charitable deed you performed, and I bow to you with reverent affection.

§34. Niccolini to Gondi (25 January 1642)[16]

This morning I saw His Holiness, seating at the usual place, but on a portable chair; he seemed to have gotten worse, and his head was so bent down that it was almost level with his shoulders. After some personal conversation, we started talking about the new Cardinal Firenzuola; His Holiness praised him as a person of great talent and intellect. He is son of the engineer who built the fortress at Palma.

On such an occasion, His Holiness remembered that Firenzuola was the Commissary of the Holy Office when the late Galileo Galilei[17] was tried by the Inquisition about his book on the earth's motion; thus, he started telling me that he wanted to share with me a particular detail, and do so in confidence and simply for the sake of conversation, not because I was supposed to report it to you. That is, His Holiness had heard that our Most Serene Ruler was thinking of having a mausoleum built for Galileo in Santa Croce, and asked me if I knew anything about it. Now, in truth, I have heard about it for many days; nevertheless, I replied that I knew nothing about it. His Holiness said that he had heard about it, but that he did not know whether it was true or false. In any case, however, he wanted to tell me that it was not a good example to the world for His Highness to do such a thing. For Galileo was tried here at the Holy Office for a very false and very erroneous opinion, of which he also convinced many other people there; and he caused a very great scandal[18] in Christendom with a doctrine that had been condemned. Then we started discussing the details of what he had been instructed to do, and of how he had admitted that he understood; and we spent a long time in those discussions.

However, I feel this is part of the duties of my office, and so I report it to Your Most Illustrious Lordship. Let me add that even if His Most Serene Highness our Ruler had such a thought regarding the memory of Mr. Galileo, I am inclined to believe that it would be better to postpone it to some other time, so as not to undergo some unpleasantness. Recall that His Holiness decided to remove the body of Countess Matilda from the Charterhouse of

---

16. Galilei 1890–1909, 18: 378–79 (no. 4196); newly translated by Finocchiaro. For further details and references, see Finocchiaro 2005, 79–85.

17. Recall that Galileo died on 8 January 1642.

18. Here the Italian reads *uno scandalo tanto universale al Cristianesimo*, which some have translated as "the greatest scandal in Christendom" (Koestler 1964; cf. 1959, 495); this alternative translation is textually less accurate, but rhetorically more effective, because in the general perception of the subsequent four centuries the responsibility appeared reversed: it was the Church herself, not Galileo, who had caused the greatest scandal in Christendom by trying and condemning him. Nevertheless, sensationalist exaggerations like Koestler's do not survive critical scrutiny; cf. Finocchiaro 2005, 306–17.

Mantua without consulting at all Lord Duke Carlo (who did not approve), and to bring it into a memorial here in Saint Peter's; he did this on the pretext that all churches belong to the pope, and that all their contents are under the jurisdiction of the Church; thus, I would not want to have to engage in long negotiations that would yield no good result.

We did not discuss any affairs of state this morning, since our time was spent on the topic mentioned above and on other personal discussions. I kiss your hands.

Index